FRANÇOIS BERTIN

D-DAY
NORMANDY
WEAPONS – UNIFORMS – MILITARY EQUIPMENT

Translation: id2m

EDITIONS OUEST-FRANCE

PREFACE

More than 60 years have past since the dark days which saw France rise from the gloomy depths of the Occupation to the jubilant heights of the Liberation in a few terrible months.

The majority of those involved in this incredibly euphoric moment in history have since left us to join the millions of civilians and soldiers who lost their lives in the greatest armed conflict the world has ever known.

Over time the scars have disappeared, emotions have calmed and memories have become clearer.

This book aims to remind readers of those summer months of 1944 with their succession of heroic accounts, destruction, courage and renunciation.

While reading this presentation of the military equipment, weapons and uniforms used by the soldiers in this immense Normandy battle, spare a thought for the men who lay behind this military façade. Men in khaki or feldgrau, from Texas, Lancashire, Quebec or Hamburg who shared the same fears, anguish and doubts day in and day out.

Regardless of their nationality, faith or political beliefs, may this book pay a final homage to these men.

Right: this Major from the German police force is sporting the specific police insignia on his left sleeve. He is wearing leather-padded riding breeches and hard boots. He is armed with a Walther PP 7.65 pistol which is strapped to his belt.

THE GERMAN OCCUPATION

D-1447

The French had to wait 1447 days for their country to be liberated. 1447 days of occupation, deprivation and humiliation before being confronted by the harsh realities of the largest military operation ever carried out.

The French government signed an armistice with Germany on 22 June 1940. While millions of French soldiers left for prisoner of war camps in Germany, France was divided into two zones by a demarcation line. The entire northern zone was occupied by German troops while the southern zone retained all of its prerogatives and preserved many of its liberties under the direct authority of the French State led by Marshall Pétain. A large strip – the forbidden zone – ran along the French coastline, from the Belgian to the Spanish border. It was in this zone (where the movement and very presence of the population was carefully watched and restricted) that thousands of structures were built which later went on to form the Atlantic Wall. On 19 August 1942, the failed raid on Dieppe by Anglo-Canadian troops reassured the Germans that they were invincible and convinced the occupied population that the landings would not be something of the near future. Following the Allied landings in North Africa on 12 November 1942, the Germans invaded the free zone. From then on the whole country was occupied and in turn, the inhabitants of the former free zone experienced the humiliation of the Occupation.

"AUSWEIS" AND CURFEW

This "Feldgendarme", or German military police officer, is dressed in a "Klepper" – a large, waterproof raincoat designed for motorcyclists but popular with all combatants. The signalling baton tucked into his belt was used by all vehicles to signal a change in direction.

He is holding a small map case in his hand and is armed with a classic 98K Mauser. He has attached the anti-mustard gas cloth carried by all infantrymen to the gas mask case that he is wearing round his neck.

The "Feldgendarme" could immediately be identified, both day and night, by the pasty-shaped plate with luminous markings that he wore round his neck and the orange piping on his epaulettes.

THE OCCUPATION

In February 1943, the Vichy government introduced forced labour (STO) to supply German factories with a workforce. Those who dodged the departures for Germany were forced to go underground and provided the Resistance movement with unexpected back-up.

Four years of occupation meant four years of hardship including, of course, loss of freedom but also many other kinds of hardship. The occupying forces lived in the country. Everything was requisitioned or seized. Equipment, raw materials, clothing, food – everything was taken to Germany or shared out among the German and foreign troops occupying the country. There were many restrictions and millions of French people became accustomed to queuing and rationing.

The Occupation also meant curfews, police roundups, arrests and bombing.

Everyone longed for the day when Allied troops would arrive and drive out the occupiers. Everyone longed for the Landings.

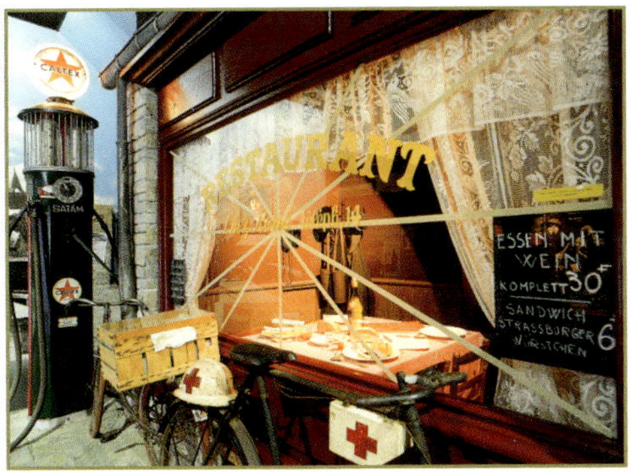

Uniform belonging to a Second Lieutenant of the Infantry

The white piping on the epaulettes and cap indicates an infantry unit. This field jacket, featuring many medals, was similar to the one worn by regular troops but of better quality for an officer. You can see the War Merit Cross 2nd Class Ribbon in the buttonhole and, below the Close Combat Bar, a ribbon bar with, from left to right, the Iron Cross 2nd Class, the Merit Cross and the Winter Battle in the East Medal.

Below the Iron Cross 1st Class, there is an Infantry Assault Badge and Gold Wound Badge.

"DER ATLANTIKWALL"

THE ATLANTIC WALL

The aim of the Atlantic Wall was to form a continuous line of defence along the west coast of France to prevent any landings. This line stretched over more than 3,000 miles from Holland to the Spanish border. Eleven million tons of concrete were used to build more than 15,000 structures, from the "Trobrukstand" – a simple foxhole – to the submarine base. Particular attention was paid to defending the northern coast (closest to England), and all the ports and fishing harbours were turned into strongholds. Both the Allied and German sides had gained experience from the Anglo-Canadian raid on Dieppe on 19 August 1942.

All along the coast that was to be the setting for Operation Overlord, the enemy lined up around thirty coastal batteries armed with four to six 105mm and 155mm guns. These batteries, often protected by concrete bunkers, were linked up by "Widerstandsnester", or nests of resistance, heavily armed for close defence and which could be grouped into bases of support, or "Stützpunkte".

ORGANISATION TODT

The Führer gave this German paramilitary organisation, run by Dr. Fritz Todt, the task of building a continuous coastal line of defence from the Dutch polders to the Spanish border. Closely supervised by German technicians, hundreds of thousands of workers, made up of volunteers and conscripts, built more than 15,000 concrete structures along the 3,000 miles of coastline. The building work, which began in December 1941, was far from finished on the morning of 6 June 1944 and the Atlantic Wall was far from being the unassailable, continuous fortress vaunted by German propaganda. Despite Field Marshall Rommel's attempts at quickly disguising the obvious weak points in the defence system, invading troops were only held up by a few hours.

The artillery, positioned all the way along the Atlantic Wall, featured guns of all calibres, and not just German guns either, as guns recovered from defeated armies were also used. French, English, Polish and Russian guns were found here, in fact the whole of Europe was represented.
From left to right, 2 Pak 37mm and 50mm anti-tank shells, then 75mm, 50mm and 37mm high explosive shells. The box of 7.92mm calibre cartridges gives an idea of their size.

BEACH DEFENCES

It was Field Marshall Edwin Rommel who was responsible for both the effectiveness of the Atlantic Wall and defending the sector most exposed to a possible landing as he was appointed Commander-in-Chief of Army Group B which covered the area from Holland to the mouth of the river Loire. At the end of 1943, aware of the inadequacies of the wall, he took many simple but effective measures such as planting stakes in the fields and flooding vast areas to prevent parachuting or landing, extending the barbed-wire fences and mine fields, and setting up anti-tank walls, trenches and all kinds of traps along the shorelines likely to be targeted by landing craft. On the eve of D-Day, the Atlantic Wall seemed to have become a reality, but not for Field Marshall Rommel, who admitted to his secretary on 22 April, "Believe me, Lang, the first twenty-four hours of the invasion will be decisive... The fate of Germany will depend on it... It will be the longest day for both the Allies and ourselves."

Bunkers

There were several types of bunker housing 20 to 210mm calibre guns served by troops from the "Heer" and "Kriegsmarine" (the German Army and Navy respectively).

Mine fields

The Germans set up a dense network of various different mines in the fields lining the beaches. The Allies countered this with mine detectors and manual mine clearance. They also used the more effective Sherman Crab Flail (a mine-clearing tank) whose chains lashed at the ground to explode the mines.

Anti-tank walls

These walls, which were sometimes several yards high and several hundred yards long, prevented tanks from advancing. To break them down, the Allies used the Pack Charge, which connected several pounds of explosive to a detonator, and a Sherman tank or "Tankdozer" fitted with a bulldozer blade at the front.

Stakes

Wedged deep in the sand, these stakes were often topped with a mine. Like the majority of beach obstacles developed by the Germans, their role was to tear open the hulls of landing craft.

Log ramps

These ramps consisted of a long log supported by two shorter logs planted in the sand. They were designed to flip the landing craft over and sometimes featured a mine at the end.

Czech hedgehogs

These were simple structures – 3 short girders welded together in the middle with one end set in a concrete block.

Belgian gates

Belgian Gates were imposing gate-like structures made from metal girders and mounted on a chassis for stability.

Barbed-wire fences

These fences covered hundreds of square yards and were reinforced with mines, grenades and booby traps. In response, the Allies resorted to the Bangalore torpedo – a piece of metal pipe filled with explosives that was slipped under the fences.

Spiked tetrahedron

This was a 3-sided pyramid made from 3 metal corner irons welded together at the ends and set on a block of concrete. Here again the aim was to bring the landing craft to a standstill and tear open their hulls.

THE PIONEERS AT THE FOOT OF THE WALL

During his last visit to Normandy in March 1944, Field Marshall Edwin Rommel was very clear. Appointed Inspector of Coastal Defences in November 1943, he was dismayed by what he saw all along the coast and immediately put a defence reinforcement plan into action. Pioneers and all available infantrymen were called upon to enlarge the mine fields, intensify the network of obstacles, plant stakes in the fields (Rommel's asparagus) to prevent planes from landing, unroll barbed-wire and set up more booby traps. Close defence of the beaches was Rommel's main concern and the creation of many WNs, or "Widerstandsnester" – autonomous and well-defended bases of support – turned out to be a major obstacle for the Allies in the first few hours of the Landings. The pioneer on the left has a special engineering bag on his back containing pliers, a knife and spanners, etc. He is wearing a "Feldmütze" 43 cap and overtrousers with splinter pattern camouflage. Armed with a 98K Mauser, he has a large pair of wire cutters tucked into his belt.

THOUSANDS OF MINES

The German anti-tank and anti-personnel Schrapnellmine 35 in its carrying case. The fuse in the centre of the device (here an anti-personnel mine), was triggered by a network of wires stretched across possible tank routes. The anti-tank mine featured a pressure-activated fuse which was triggered by the weight of the vehicle. This mine measures 12 inches in diameter and is 3 inches thick. It was found, complete with case, in a buried bunker at the Pointe du Hoc in Normandy.

MADE OF CONCRETE, WOOD OR GLASS...

The Germans set up a dense network of mines to reinforce their defences on the beaches and adjacent land. To prevent them from being detected and consequently defused, these explosive devices were made from non-magnetic material such as wood, glass or concrete.

Left, a glass mine.

A thin sheet of glass was covered by a coloured, pressed sheet of glass. This was then placed above the detonator which was positioned above a stick of TNT in a jar. Such a device was virtually undetectable. The thin sheet of glass would break under the slightest pressure, crushing the detonator and triggering the explosion.

Right, a concrete mine.

These mines were cast in concrete and were also difficult to detect. They were filled with small, steel balls and were often mounted on a buried wooden post. The traction detonator was visible at the top of the mine. A network of almost invisible wires connected up the detonator making the mine difficult to locate and defuse. These two types of mine claimed many victims both during the fighting and during mine clearing operations mainly carried out by German POWs at the end of the war.

GERMAN SOLDIERS' MILITARY EQUIPMENT

This belt, belonging to a Luftwaffe infantryman, features 98K rifle cartridge pouches and an 84/98 bayonet scabbard. Each grainy black leather cartridge pouch held 2 x 5 cartridge magazines.

The regulation gas mask was carried in a fluted metal box. Spare eyepieces (seen here in their glassine envelope) were stored in the cap. The mask strap has the same name as the box – "Schutz" (infantryman) Jessen Herman, followed by the number 545.

Heer soldier

The white piping on the epaulettes indicates an infantry soldier from the Heer. During his military career, this solider received the General Assault Badge, the Sports Badge, the Wound Badge and he is wearing the Iron Cross 2nd Class Ribbon in his buttonhole.

The 1931 bread bag was often used by soldiers to carry both bread and personal items. In addition to the regulation cap – the "Feldmütze" – here you can see a compact alcohol burner, a glasses case marked "Dienst-Brille", a sewing kit marked "Nadeln", a rifle repair kit, a razor, the traditional orange butter dish and some cutlery.

A 3-colour camouflaged helmet from the Kriegsmarine which can be distinguished by the special shape of the eagle on the left side. This helmet almost certainly belonged to a soldier from a coastal unit defending the Atlantic Wall. It was found on the Normandy coast close to Ver-sur-Mer.

Regulation Wehrmacht back pack, or "cowhide". The contents of the 1934 back-pack were protected by a cloth flap covered in calf hide. Soldiers used this pack to carry a pair of boots, a toilet bag, a mess tin and cover, and emergency provisions.

This infantry-man, who is wearing the combat pack adopted in 1939, is armed with a 98K Mauser rifle.

Equipment was dropped by the container load into the maquis. These metal containers, measuring nearly 2 yards in length, were made up of detachable casks and contained all the equipment required for a war of subversion – weapons, ammunition, explosives, transmission equipment, provisions, etc.

Musée de Saint-Marcel collection

GREEN PLAN, TORTOISE PLAN AND PURPLE PLAN

Three destruction plans were passed on to the Maquis (French Resistance fighters). The Green plan involved sabotaging the railway lines to prevent troops, equipment and especially tanks from being transported to the landing areas. As its name suggests, the Tortoise plan targeted the road network and the Purple plan, the telephone lines. Together these three plans aimed to create confusion among the German troops and make a counter-attack difficult or even impossible.

THE RESISTANCE IN NORMANDY

English agents sent radio transceivers hidden in suitcases to some Resistance groups so that they could communicate with London.

D-1/7.40pm

"...wound my heart with a monotonous languor."

The Germans did hear this personal message from the BBC, taken from one of Verlaine's verses, and 48 hours beforehand radio monitors from the 15th German Army had caught the first part of the verse "The long sobs/Of autumn's violins...". They knew that, on hearing the second part, the Landings were imminent but the officers of the units in Normandy were never informed of this. In the meantime, the BBC broadcast personal messages to the Maquis – "The dice are on the carpet", "It's hot in Suez", etc. Resistance groups in Normandy and the rest of France immediately sabotaged telephone lines, blew up railway lines and blocked roads by cutting down trees. Now disorganised and worried, the Germans also had to endure the intensive bombing of their line of defence.

Resistance fighters naturally had to make do with a mismatch of arms. Allied weapons – English Enfield rifle, American M1 carbine and Colt 45 pistol – were used alongside those seized from the enemy – MP40 sub-machine gun, MG34 machine gun, grenades, etc.

A Maquis pennant and US M1-A1 carbine with a folding metal butt and Maquis emblem carved by its owner.
(Musée de la Résistance collection, Saint-Marcel).

DISTINGUISHING BETWEEN THE WAFFEN-SS AND THE HEER

The distinctive yellow piping on these caps indicates armoured reconnaissance units. Left, an Waffen-SS cap, identifiable by its skull and crossbones. Right, a Heer cap.

TANK CREWS

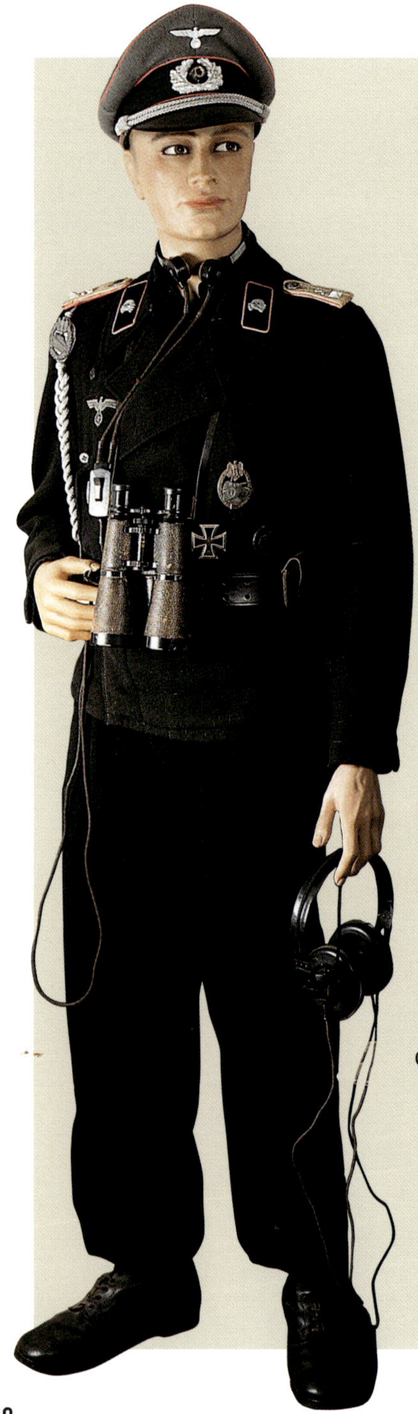

Heer Panzerdivision crews wore the same uniform as the SS Panzerdivison crews – the same black woollen cloth uniform and black boots. Their caps were noticeably different however. The SS cap had a skull and crossbones on the cap band while the army tank teams had a cockade and the traditional oak leaves. Their lapels were also different. SS Panzerdivison crews wore the SS runes on the right and the specific rank on the left while Heer crews had a skull and crossbones on a black rectangle with pink piping on each lapel. The belt buckles are also obviously different.

The widespread use of camouflaged uniforms and the fact that some items on their uniforms were inspired by the same symbols, for instance, the skull and crossbones on a black background, meant that it was sometimes difficult to distinguish a Heer infantryman from an SS Panzerdivison grenadier.

INFANTRYMEN

Like the tank crews, Waffen-SS infantrymen wore the eagle specific to their service on their left sleeve. As for the helmets, you could either find the SS runes on a black or white shield, or the Wehrmacht eagle.

Camouflage smocks worn over the uniforms often prevented precise identification. As the helmets were often completely covered with camouflage paint, only the lapels on the tunic worn underneath the smock could be used to identify the soldiers. Their weapons and equipment were identical.

THE HUGE 6,939-STRONG ARMADA SETS SAIL

The fighting squadron
7 battleships
23 cruisers
221 destroyers, frigates and corvettes
495 gunboats
58 submarine chasers
4 mine layers
2 submarines

The logistic fleet
736 auxiliary vessels
864 freighters

The landing force
4,126 ships and landing craft divided up into 47 convoys

229 LSTs (Landing Ship Tank)
They were able to transport up to 2,000 tons of men and equipment, and 2 to 6 LCVPs. They were armed with one 40mm gun and six 20mm guns. There were also LST (Hospital) ships. Crew:100. Length: 323ft.

245 LCIs (Landing Craft Infantry)
They carried up to 200 men.
Length: 153ft.

911 LCTs (Landing Craft Tank)
They carried tanks, which were not fitted out for an amphibious attack, and "tankdozers". Crew: 13. Length (version 5): 111ft. Length (version 6): 115ft.

481 LCMs (Landing Craft, Mechanised)
Varying in weight and size, they were able to carry one tank. Crew: 4. Length: 49ft.

1,089 LCVPs (Landing Craft Vehicle, Personnel)
They carried 30 men or one small vehicle. Crew: 3. Length: 36ft.

Naval armament
The armada also featured powerful battleships.
Force 0:
U.S.S. *Texas* (10 x 350mm, 6 x 125mm and 10 x 75mm), U.S.S. *Arkansas* (12 x 300mm and 10 x 75mm), U.S.S. *Augusta* (9 x 200mm and 8 x 125mm).
Force U:
U.S.S. *Nevada* (10 x 350mm and 16 x 125mm), U.S.S. *Quincy* (9 x 200mm and 12 x 125mm), U.S.S. *Tuscaloosa* (9 x 200 and 8 x 125mm).

D-385

CODE NAME: "OVERLORD"

It was during the Trident Conference, held in Washington in May 1943, that the Allies set a date for the Landings in France. They decided on 1 May 1944 in Pas-de-Calais or the Baie de Seine and they code-named the operation "Overlord". Two important decisions were then made in Quebec in August of the same year. Firstly, the Landings would take place on the Calvados coastline, along a 50-mile stretch which included the Cotentin peninsula and the port of Cherbourg. Secondly, due to resources, the date of the operation was put back to the morning of 5 June with the option of delaying the operation still further by 1 or 2 days.

The American sector

The Anglo-Canadian sector

SHAEF

(SUPREME HEADQUARTERS ALLIED EXPEDITIONARY FORCE)

ALLIED COMMAND

General Command

- Supreme Commander Allied Expeditionary Force
  General Dwight Eisenhower
- Deputy Supreme Commander
  Air Chief Marshal A.W. Tedder
- Commander-in-chief Allied Expeditionary Force
  Air Chief Marshal T. Leigh-Mallory
- Commander-in-Chief Land Forces
  B.L. Montgomery, Commanding Officer 21st Army Group
- Commander-in-Chief Allied Expeditionary Naval Force
  Admiral B.H. Ramsay

American Landing Troop Command

- Commanding Officer 1st US Army
  Lieutenant General Omar N. Bradley

Utah Sector

- 7th Corps Major General J.L. Collins

Omaha Sector

- 5th Corps Major General L.T. Gerow

British and Canadian Landing Troop Command

- Commander 2nd British Army
  Lieutenant General M.C. Dempsey

Gold Sector

- 30th Corps Lieutenant General G.C. Bucknall

Juno and Sword Sectors

- 1st Corps Lieutenant General J.T. Crocker

Heer
Infantry officer's cap with the Wehrmacht eagle, cockade and white piping.

Kriegsmarine
Cap belonging to an officer from the coastal artillery who was responsible to the German Navy. The cap features the German Navy's eagle and cockade.

Panzer
Heer Panzer officer's cap with the pink piping specific to the tank crews.

Artillery
Cap belonging to a non-commissioned officer from the Artillery with the red piping of the Artillery

Luftwaffe
Cap belonging to a non-commissioned officer from the Luftwaffe with the German Air Force's eagle and cockade.

Waffen-SS
Cap belonging to an officer from the Waffen-SS Panzer division with the Waffen-SS eagle, skull and crossbones and the tank crew pink piping.

LYING IN WAIT D-1 / 8.30pm

Artillerymen, tank crews, infantrymen and airmen were all waiting for the Landings. In barracks and thousands of bunkers dotted along the Normandy coastline, the German troops, armed and ready with their binoculars fixed on the horizon, were on the lookout for that unavoidable moment, when, as Field Marshall Rommel said, they would have a day to drive back the enemy. For both the Germans and the Allies, this was going to be the longest day.

OB/WEST

GERMAN COMMAND

ARMEEGRUPPE B

Feldmarschall Erwin Rommel

- **7th Army** / General F. Dollmann
  - **84th Corps** / General Marcks
    - 716th Infantry Division
    - 352nd Infantry Division
    - 709th Infantry Division
    - 243rd Infantry Division
    - 319th Infantry Division
    - 91st Infantry Division

  Reserve troops:
    - 21st Panzer Division
    - 22nd Panzer Regiment
    - 125th Panzer Grenadier
    - 192nd Panzer Grenadier
    - 155th Panzer Grenadier
    - 21st Armoured Reconnaissance Detachment
    - 200th Tank Chaser Detachment
    - 220th Armoured Pioneer Battalion
    - 116th Panzer Division
    - 2nd Panzer Division

- **15th Army** / General H. von Salmuth
  - **81st Corps**

German units in Normandy

Rommel requested that the tanks from the 12th SS Panzer Division "Hitlerjugend" and "Panzer Lehr", stationed a long way south of Caen, be brought closer to the coast. Luckily for the Allies, on 6 June 1944 this request was still making its way to the Führer – the only person authorised to move the armoured divisions. A wide range of units lined the coast directly concerned by the Landings and the Allies lacked information as to the efficiency of each individual unit. Therefore, it was not a unit of tired veterans which awaited the Americans on Omaha Beach but a very experienced infantry division (352nd).

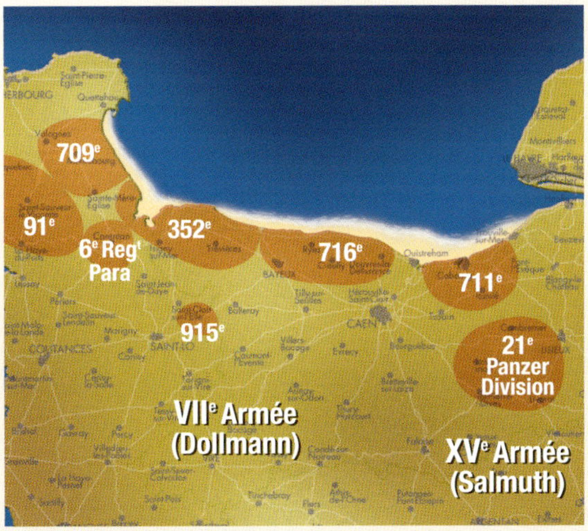

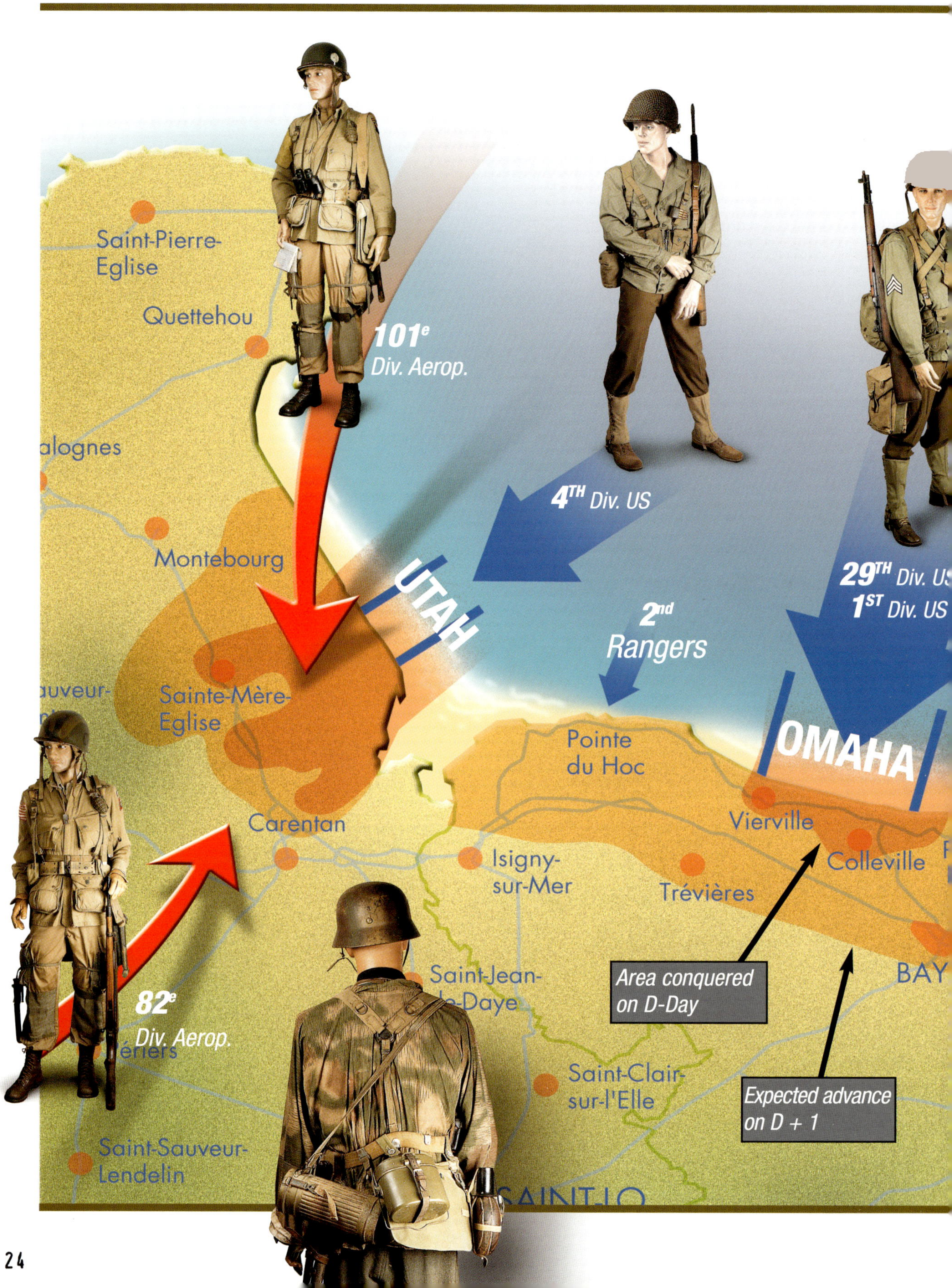
Saint-Pierre-Eglise
Quettehou
alognes
Montebourg
auveur-
Sainte-Mère-Eglise
Carentan
Isigny-sur-Mer
Pointe du Hoc
Vierville
Colleville
Trévières
Saint-Jean-de-Daye
Saint-Clair-sur-l'Elle
Saint-Sauveur-Lendelin
ériers
SAINT-LO
BAY
101e Div. Aerop.
82e Div. Aerop.
4TH Div. US
2nd Rangers
29TH Div. US
1ST Div. US
UTAH
OMAHA
Area conquered on D-Day
Expected advance on D + 1

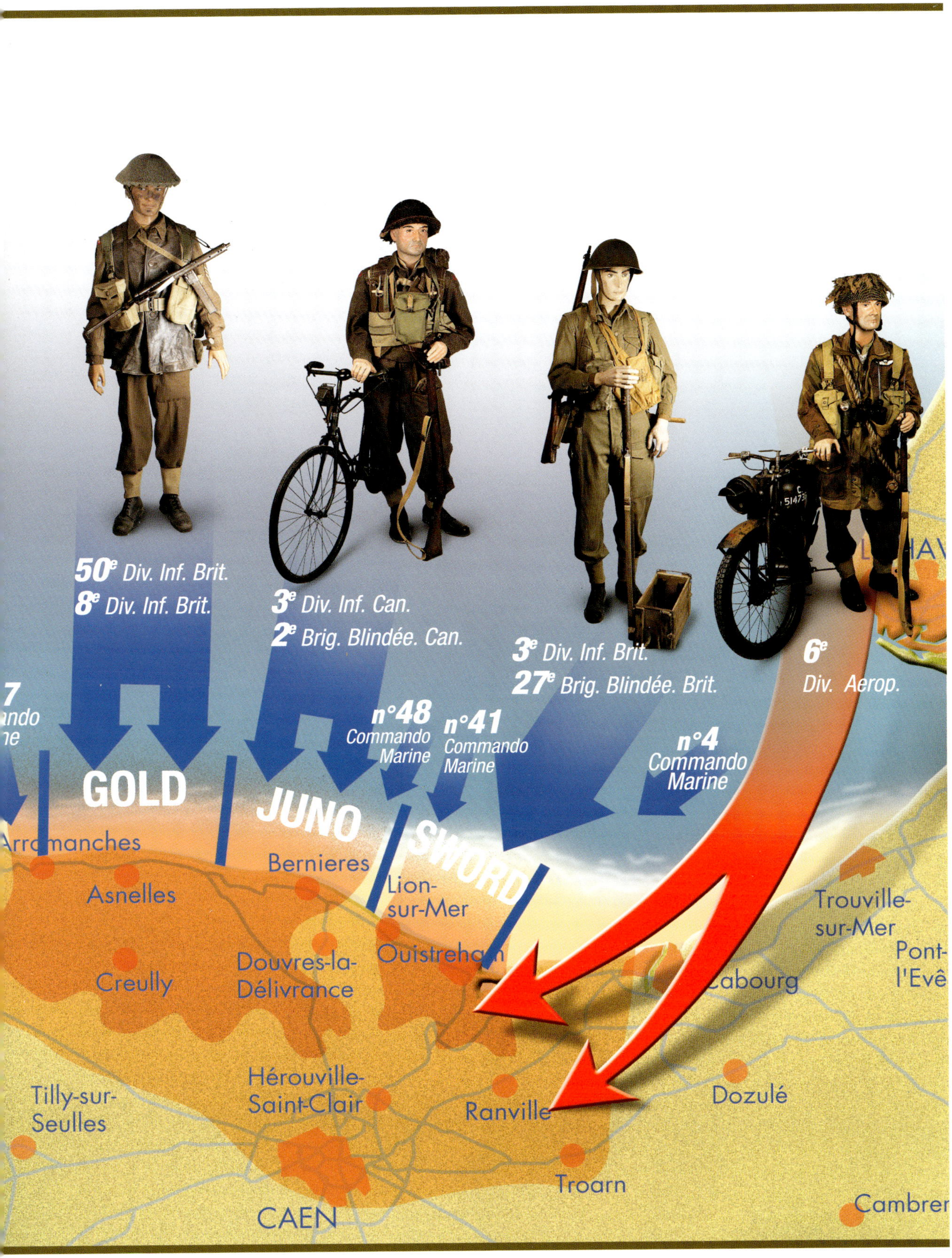
50e Div. Inf. Brit.
8e Div. Inf. Brit.
3e Div. Inf. Can.
2e Brig. Blindée. Can.
3e Div. Inf. Brit.
27e Brig. Blindée. Brit.
6e Div. Aerop.
n°48 Commando Marine
n°41 Commando Marine
n°4 Commando Marine
GOLD
JUNO
SWORD
Asnelles
Bernieres
Lion-sur-Mer
Ouistreham
Douvres-la-Délivrance
Creully
Trouville-sur-Mer
Hérouville-Saint-Clair
Ranville
Dozulé
Tilly-sur-Seulles
Troarn
CAEN

SOLDIER FROM THE 1ST CANADIAN PARACHUTE BATTALION

This paratrooper is wearing a Denison smock and Pattern 1937 web equipment (with cartridge pouches) over his BD tunic. You can just about make out the regulation string vest around his neck. The press studs at the bottom of the smock were used to attach the "tail piece" or "ape tail" during the parachute jump. The paratrooper has a "Toggle rope" over his shoulder which, when linked to other ropes, was used to scale walls, etc. He is armed with a No. 4 Mark 1 Rifle with a spike bayonet. His uniform is identical to the one worn by the British paratroopers – the yellow loop on his epaulettes is the only indication of his Canadian nationality. He is holding a James ML motorbike, with a Villiers 125cc 2-stroke engine, designed specifically for airborne troops. Notice that unlike their American colleagues, British and Canadian paratroopers did not carry a reserve parachute. This decision was justified at the time by the fact that equipment was expensive and that jumps were made at such low altitudes that reserve chutes were not effective.

D / 0.16am

Major Howard's paratroopers attack Benouville Bridge

The British 6th Airborne Division was assigned the area between the Orne and Dives rivers to protect the eastern side of the Landing beaches by neutralising German batteries (such as the one in Merville) and destroying certain bridges while leaving others intact (such as Benouville Bridge). At 0.16am, the first of three gliders landed on the river bank, just a few yards from the bridge held by the Germans who were oblivious to it all. The attack therefore came as a complete surprise and the target was rapidly secured by the D company of the 2nd Battalion Ox and Bucks, led by Major Howard, which held the bridge until the arrival of men from the 1st Commando who landed on Sword Beach in the early hours of the morning. Although the

A paratrooper's steel airborne troop helmet on a Bergman metal-framed bag. Originally designed for mountain troops, it was later given to other units operating without logistic support. In the foreground, a Sten Mk V "Airborne Troop" 9mm parabellum sub-machine gun – a model specifically designed for paratroopers with its wooden butts. Some soldiers removed the rear butt to make the gun easier to handle.

THE 6TH AIRBORNE DIVISION

- ***3rd Parachute Brigade***
  - 8th Battalion Parachute Regiment
  - 9th Battalion Parachute Regiment
  - 1st Canadian Parachute Battalion
- ***5th Parachute Brigade***
  - 7th Battalion Parachute Regiment
  - 12th Battalion Parachute Regiment
  - 13th Battalion Parachute Regiment
- ***6th Air Landing Brigade***
  - 2nd Airborne Battalion The Oxfordshire and Buckinghamshire Light Infantry (Ox and Bucks)
  - 1st Airborne Battalion The Royal Ulster Rifles
  - 12th Airborne Battalion The Devonshire Regiment (A Company)
- ***Divisional Troops***
  - 22nd Independent Company Parachute Regiment (pathfinders)
  - 6th Airborne Armoured Regiment Reconnaissance Corps – Royal Armoured Corps
  - 53rd Air Landing Light Regiment – Royal Artillery
  - 1st and 2nd Squadrons of the Glider Pilot Regiment
  - Royal Engineers, Royal Corps of Signals and Army Medical Corps Parachute Regiments
- ***Troops attached to the 6th Airborne Division***
  - No. 3, No. 4 and No. 6 Commando of the 1st Special Service Battalion
  - 45 Royal Marine Commando

THE FIRST ALLIED SOLDIER KILLED ON D-DAY

Lieutenant Brotheridge, who was under the orders of Major John Howard, took part in the attack on the Benouville bridge garrison alongside his men. He was fatally injured by enemy fire while leading the attack on the bridge.

6TH AIRBORNE

The mission of the British and Canadian paratroopers from the 6th Airborne Division was to protect the right side of the Landing beaches. They had to secure an entire area to prevent an attack from German troops stationed further east. This buffer zone was located inland, between the river Dives and the mouth of the Orne which flows through Caen.

This British paratrooper's helmet comes from Ranville. The words "R. Watson Pret Amcorp" were marked on the inside liner by the owner.

"sticks" were spread over a wide area and much heavy equipment was lost, the British and Canadian paratroopers reached their assigned targets. The dangerous Merville battery was captured by men from Lt. Col. Otway's 9th Battalion and the five bridges spanning the river Dives were destroyed by the British 8th Battalion and 1st Canadian Battalion thus preventing any German incursion into the eastern side of the Allied defence system.

Resting on a British paratrooper's lifebelt, from left to right: Fairbain dagger, short Toggle Rope and in the foreground, new and old model paratrooper regimental cap badges.

PARATROOPER FROM THE 6TH AIRBORNE DIVISION

This paratrooper is wearing the famous airborne troop maroon beret, complete with the Parachute Regiment badge. He has a handgun holster on his Pattern 37 web belt and the gun wrist strap is attached to his left epaulette. Note, under the Denison smock, the large pocket on left leg of his BD trousers. He is resting on an ammunition carrying case.

6th Airborne Division's landing zones

DZ (Dropping Zone) "V" / *Varaville*
Mission assigned to the 9th Battalion and the 1st Canadian Battalion
DZ "K" / *Touffréville*
Mission assigned to the 9th Battalion
DZ "N" / *Ranville*
Mission assigned to the 7th, 13th and 12th Battalions
LZ (Landing Zone) "X" and LZ "Y"/ *river Orne and canal*
Mission assigned to the D Company of the 2nd Battalion Ox and Bucks and a platoon of the 249th Field Company
LZ "W" / *Saint-Aubin-d'Arguenay*
Operation Mallard: 9pm mission assigned to the 6th Air Landing Brigade.

"ALARM, ALARM!... SIE KOMMEN!..."

This Heer Signal Corps soldier, wearing the standard uniform, is carrying a battle pack and radio set on his back. He has headphones around his neck and communicates via a throat microphone – the small control box can be seen on the brown strap.

D / 1.30am

General Marcks, commanding the 84th Corps of the German Army, is informed of the first landings by parachute

As the information came from several sources at once and was unclear, and as it was difficult to contact the units concerned, the officers working alongside General Marcks found it hard to assess the situation. It was initially believed that these "famous" paratroopers were in fact only dummies made from potato sacks. Until, that was, the first British and American paratroopers taken prisoner arrived at the headquarters and cast doubt over this belief. At 3.10am, Admiral Hennecke sent out a few fast patrol boats from Cherbourg having been alerted of suspicious engine noises out to sea by his listening stations. But these boats came back with nothing to report. The Wehrmacht, Kriegsmarine and Luftwaffe officers were all puzzled but they were also all convinced of at least one thing – the Landings (or the Invasion as they referred to it) could only take place in the Pas-de-Calais and nowhere else.

A German field telephone in its Bakelite case. The detachable crank on the right was used to power the magneto supplying the electric current. In addition to the handset inside the case, the telephone could also be used with individual headphones.

Dimensions:
Length: 10.5 inches
Width: 9 inches
Depth: 3.5 inches

D / 1.49am

Men from the 101st Airborne Division under General Taylor land on Sainte-Marie-du-Mont

Like their comrades from the 82nd Airborne Division, the mission of the 6,600 paratroopers from the 101st Airborne Division was to protect the west side of the Landing beaches. The 432 Dakota C-47 planes carrying the paratroopers had been preceded by pathfinders who had been dropped an hour before to mark out the drop zones and secure the ground. Heavy Flak gunfire combined with the weather conditions meant that the sticks landed miles apart and regrouping was therefore difficult. Much of the heavy equipment was lost. Throughout the night, small groups of disorientated paratroopers searched for fellow troops along the sunken lanes, shooting at the rare German detachments trying to get a clearer picture of the situation. On the whole, the missions assigned to the 101st Airborne Division were carried out successfully by the evening of D-Day.

THE 101ST AIRBORNE DIVISION "SCREAMING EAGLES"

The "Screaming Eagle" emblem consisted of an eagle's head on a black shield. The bald eagle is the national bird of the United States.

The US 101st Airborne Division
General Maxwell Taylor

- 501st, 502nd and 506th Parachute Infantry Regiments
- 377th Parachute Field Artillery Battalion
- 327th Glider Infantry Regiment
- 321st and 907th Glider Field Artillery Battalion
- 326th Airborne Engineer Battalion

It was customary for paratroopers to attach their parachute first aid pouch to the top of their helmets. It was tied to the camouflage net using laces. This net also had British-inspired coloured strips of cloth.

Found in the Montebourg area, this jump coat belonged to Chief Sergeant Reoden, a 6th June Pathfinder. The jacket, which pathfinders felt was too pale, has been camouflaged (including the rank badge) by large bands of green paint. The rope around the neck is a Toggle Rope, something often used by British paratroopers to scale walls, build temporary ladders, bridges, etc.

Musée Omaha, Saint-Laurent-sur-Mer collection.

This Technician 5th Grade from the 101st A/B Div. is carrying his revolver in a special holster which was also used by armoured units and sometimes even adopted by officers.

A Paratrooper Officer from the 101st Airborne Division, the "Screaming Eagles"

The white marking on his M1C helmet indicates that he belongs to the 377th Parachute Field Artillery Battalion. The cloth chin strap has been hooked up at the back. He has a sleeve gas detector on his right sleeve and under the map case slung over his shoulder you can see the handle of a small M-1943 folding entrenching tool.
His M3 trench knife is in a US M8 vulcanised-cloth scabbard which is strapped to his right calf. His belt features a cloth pouch for two US M1 carbine magazines. He is wearing an M-1942 jump uniform made up of trousers with two cargo pockets and a 4-pocket tunic which is drawn in around the waist. Cargo pocket contents were kept in place by a tied strap. The strap you can see around the left knee belongs to the gas mask case.

101st Airborne Division's landing zones

DZ "A" / Saint-Martin-de-Varreville
Mission assigned to the 502nd Parachute Infantry Regiment and the 377th Parachute Field Artillery Battalion.
DZ "C" / Hiesville
Mission assigned to the 3rd Company of the 501st Parachute Infantry Regiment, 1st and 2nd Companies of the 506th Parachute Infantry Regiment and the HQ of the 101st Airborne Division.
DZ "D" / Angoville-au-Plain
Mission assigned to the 1st and 2nd Companies of the 501st Parachute Infantry Regiment, the 3rd Company of the 506th Parachute Infantry Regiment and the C Company of the 326th Airborne Engineer Battalion.
LZ "E" / Hiesville
Mission Chicago: D / 4am
Mission Keokuck: D / 9pm

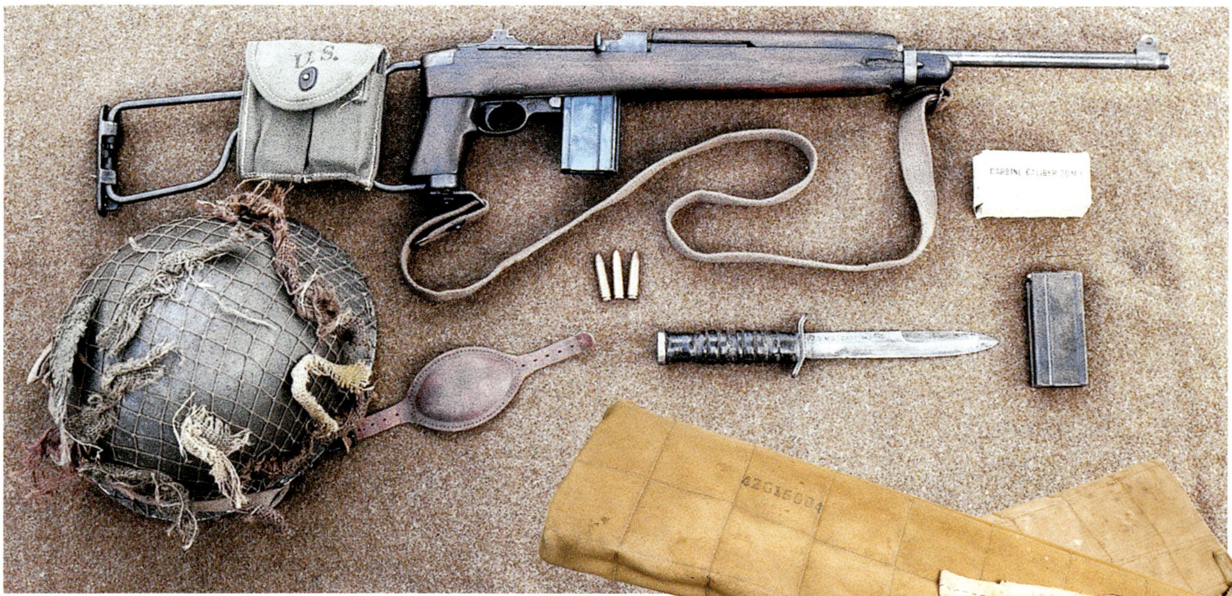

The US M1A1 carbine has a double magazine pouch attached to the folding metal butt. To the right of the M1C helmet with leather chin strap, an M3 dagger

To carry the M1 Garand rifle or M1 carbine in complete safety, paratrooper units were equipped with padded covers. In the foreground, the machete was used both as a weapon and a tool.

Unlike the main parachute, opened by an automatic strap connected to the plane, the reserve parachute featured a handle which could be pulled in the event of a faulty main canopy. This manoeuvre was made risky by the relatively low altitude at which the jumps were made and also by the darkness. The reserve chute was attached to the harness loops by two clasps. Only American paratroopers carried a reserve chute.

Each parachute carried a small "Parachute log record" in a specially-sewn pocket. Parachute no. 104 fulfilled its task on the night of the 5th/6th June 1944. In the foreground, a wrist compass and the first aid pouch that the paratroopers often carried strapped to the camouflage net on their helmets.

This paratrooper helmet is not camouflaged. The lighter band of paint on the top of the helmet was used to warn others of the presence of poison gas. The regimental number W 9101 has been painted on the liner. The black circle that you can just about make out on the left side was a specific unit mark.

On the night of 6 June 1944, American paratroopers jumped with their T5 parachute back packs worn over lifejackets which could only be inflated once the cumbersome harness (which featured at least 3 clasps) had been unfastened and such a manoeuvre was often hampered further by enemy fire. This paratrooper has the letter "G" and a flash of lightening stencilled on the left side of the lifejacket. This stood for "Geronimo", which the men from the 508th Parachute Infantry Regiment cried out as they jumped from the plane. The 60sq. yd. parachute canopy was made from Nylon with a yellow and green camouflage pattern.

PARATROOPER FROM THE 82ND AIRBORNE DIVISION

To the right of the German rifle that this soldier is holding, you can see the old M-1910 T-handle entrenching tool which was still issued to some airborne units. He is wearing fawn-coloured leather gloves like those worn by the cavalry. An M3 trench knife in an M6 leather scabbard is strapped to his right calf. He is wearing the famous cricket round his neck – a small metal toy which was handed out on the eve of D-Day and used by paratroopers to identify themselves and recognise others in the night. This paratrooper has also sewn a cloth or muslin American flag on his right sleeve (these flags were distributed at the same time as the crickets). The pockets on his beige poplin cotton parachute jumper coat are filled to the brim. Note that the coat elbows and trouser knees have been reinforced with strips of sewn cloth. He is also wearing rubber-soled, brown chrome leather parachute jump boots.

The 82nd Airborne Division's landing zones

DZ "O" */ Sainte-Mère-Eglise*
Mission assigned to the 505th Parachute Infantry Regiment and the HQ of the 82nd Airborne Division
DZ "T" */ Amfreville*
Mission assigned to the 507th Parachute Infantry Regiment
DZ "N" */ Picauville*
Mission assigned to the 508th Parachute Infantry Regiment and the B Company of the 307th Airborne Engineer Battalion
LZ "W" */ Les Forges*
Mission Elmira: 9pm
Mission Galveston: D-Day + 1 / 7am
Hackensack: D-Day + 1 / 9am
LZ "O" */ Sainte-Mère-Eglise*
Mission Detroit: 4am

D / 1.51am

The 505th Parachute Infantry Regiment of the 82nd Airborne Division under General Ridgeway lands on Sainte-Mère-Eglise

The 82nd Airborne Division drop zone lay either side of Merderet, a marshy area which the Allies believed to be free from major obstacles but which the Germans had partly flooded just a few days before. It was a complete disaster – the men drowned within minutes, weighed down by the tens of pounds of equipment they were carrying. The 505th Parachute Infantry Regiment escaped death by landing virtually on its target – the small village of Sainte-Mère-Eglise which it quickly surrounded. At 4.30am, the 3rd Battalion commander, Lt. Col. Edward C. Krause, was able to officially announce the capture of the small village. Out of the 13,000 men enlisted in the two divisions, more than 2,500 were put out of action having been reported killed, wounded or missing.

The generals jumped with their men…

Brigadier General James M. Gavin was deputy to Major General Matthew B. Ridgway, Commander of the 82nd Airborne Division.

Musée Airborne collection, Sainte-Mère-Eglise

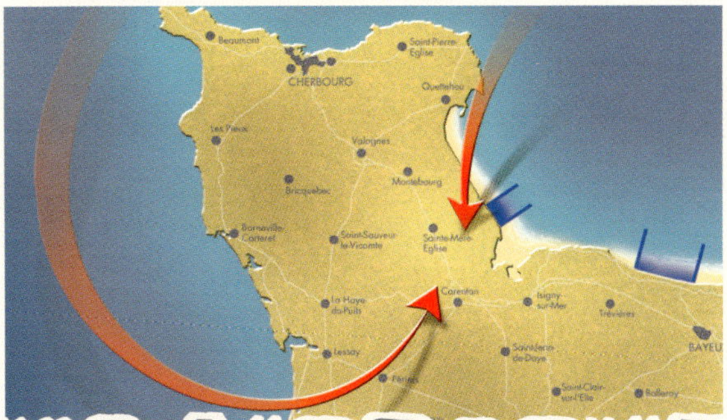

US AIRBORNE

The mission assigned to the American paratroopers was to capture and secure a vast area near the Cotentin Peninsula, to the left of the most western Landing beach. This area covered almost 50 square miles inland of Utah Beach. The paratroopers were preceded by 120 pathfinders, only 38 of whom were able to successfully complete their mission.

THE 82ND AIRBORNE "ALL AMERICAN" DIVISION

The division's emblem comprised two white "A"s in a blue circle on a red rectangle – the colours of the American flag. The two "A"s stood for "All American". The 82nd Airborne Division brought together newly formed regiments which integrated immediately.

US 82nd Airborne Division
General Ridgeway

- 505th, 507th and 508th Parachute Infantry Regiments
- 376th Parachute Field Artillery Battalion
- 325th Glider Infantry Regiment
- 319th Airborne Field Artillery Regiment
- 307th Airborne Engineer Battalion

Precise organisation

Each landing craft held a certain number of infantrymen organised according to their specific missions and weapons. Each man had a very precise function and position in the craft. For the Omaha and Utah Beach landings, the 30 men on board were organised in two different ways. First came the Assault Boat Team made up of riflemen and support weapons, and then, a few minutes later, the Support Boat Team which carried the battalion's heavy weapons.

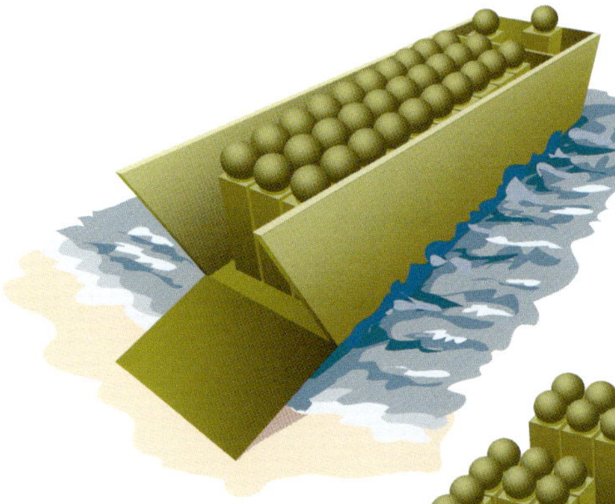

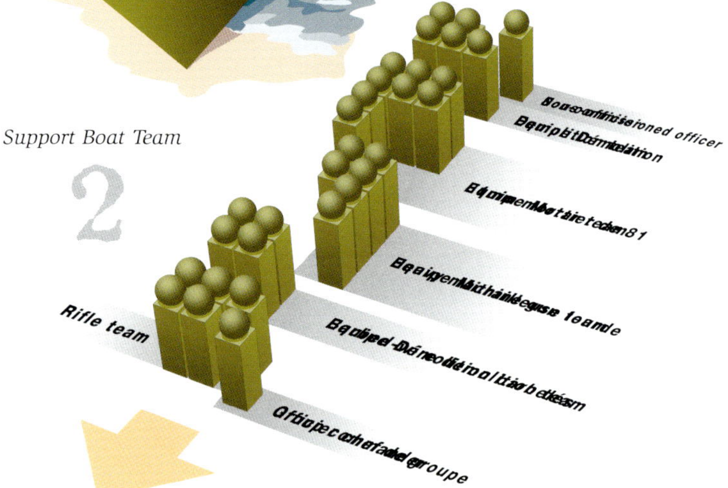

From the LCVP to the LST

The landing fleet was made up of a wide range of vessels from the smallest – the 36ft. long LCVP which carried 30 men – to the LST, an incredible 328ft. long liner which could unload more than 2,000 tons of cargo on to the beaches in one go.

Number of boats used in the British and Americans sectors:
1,089 LCVPs, 481 LCMs, 911 LCTs, 245 LCIs and 229 LSTs.

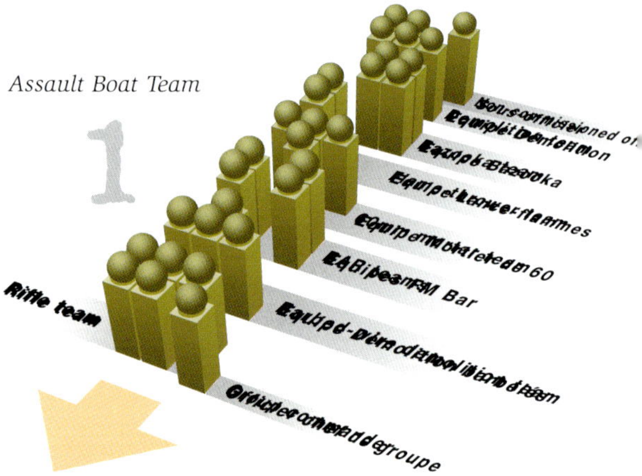

LCVP Landing Craft Vehicle, Personnel
36 men or 1 vehicle

LCM Landing Craft, Mechanised
1 light tank or 1 truck

LCT Landing Craft Tank
4 DD tanks and vehicles or 7 Sherman tanks

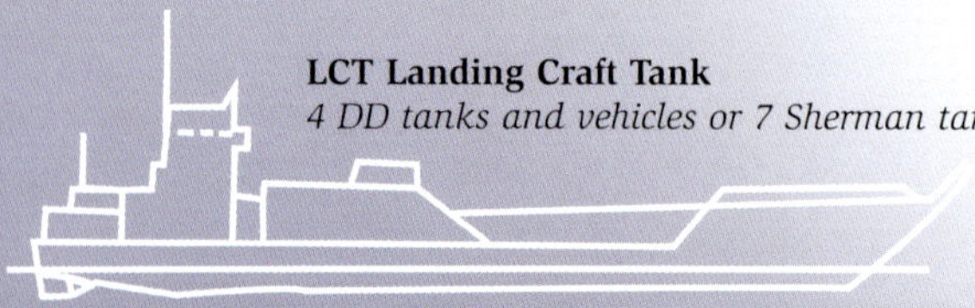

LCI Landing Craft Infantry
188 men (an infantry company)

LST Landing Ship Tank
2,000 tons (men and equipment) and 2 to 6 LCVPs.

D / 4am

The first troops left the carriers to board the landing craft...

During the night of 5/6 June 1944, the sea was very rough and soldiers not accustomed to life at sea suffered terribly. Many were badly seasick and when the time came to leave the landing craft they were in no fit state to launch an attack. And yet the infantrymen had crossed the Channel aboard large ships.

The Landing beach guardian angels
Besides piloting a large number of landing ships, the American Coast Guards were deployed throughout Operation Overlord in sixty 62ft. long patrol boats, specifically fitted out to come to the rescue of soldiers in trouble. 1,483 men were therefore saved from drowning by the Coast Guard Rescue Flotilla One.

LCVO OR LCA

The landing craft, which led the first waves of assault, were mainly LCVPs (Landing Craft Vehicle Personnel) on the American side and LCAs (Landing Craft Assault) on the British side. The LCVP, which was more sturdy and open, was made entirely of metal while the LCA, which featured a gunwale, was made from marine plywood and partly protected by armoured plating. Each craft carried about forty men.

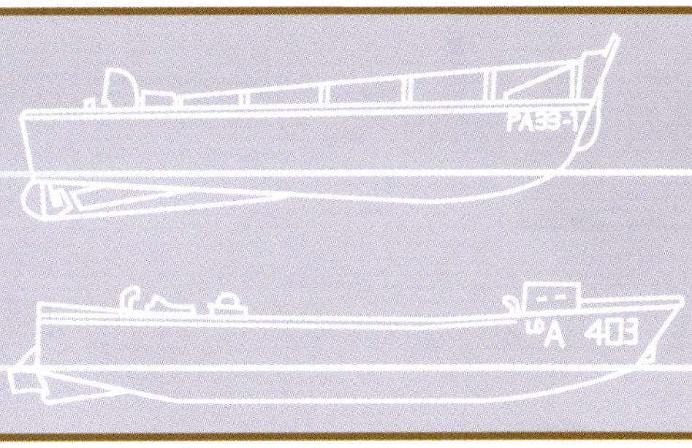

The LCM (Landing Craft Mechanised) could carry a light tank which it delivered straight on to the beach using its mobile ramp. Here the LCM is carrying a Sherman tank fitted with air-intake ducts which enabled it to move along the sea bed with the turret level with the water. This is not to be confused with a Sherman DD or Duplex Drive which was fitted with an inflatable skirt and actually floated on the water.

GI UNIFORM

1 – M1 steel helmet covered with a camouflage net.
2 – Adjustable, fibranne liner
3 – HBT (Herring Bone Twill) jacket
4 – Mustard wool trousers
5 – M1 Garand semi-automatic rifle
6 – On the M-1923 cartridge belt: metal water bottle and cloth cover, cloth first aid pouch, bayonet and scabbard
7 – M-1928 haversack and pack carrier
8 – M-1910 T-handle entrenching tool
9 – Leather laced boots with lace-up cloth gaiters

All items of clothing were treated with an anti-vesicant gas product.

D / 6.30am

The first waves of assault from the 4th US Infantry Division reach Utah Beach

The mission of the VIIth Corps, which included the 4th US Infantry Division, was to land on Utah Beach and capture the port of Cherbourg. The first wave of assault was made up of the 1st and 2nd Battalions of the 8th Infantry Regiment which landed on time but ended up 2,000 yards south of the targeted area. General Theodore Roosevelt decided to land all his men here and the waves of men and equipment continued throughout the day without much opposition from the enemy. The 22nd Infantry Regiment crossed the dunes and marshland to reach its initial targets and link up with paratroopers from the 101st Airborne who had been holding the inland area since the night before. Units from the 82nd Airborne units landed and met up with their comrades in Sainte-Mère-Eglise. The 4th Infantry Division lost 197 men in the operation, a relatively modest figure in view of the tragic Omaha Beach death toll.

4TH DIVISION

The 4th Division badge comprised 4 ivy leaves in the shape of a cross. There was a simple explanation for this. The number four in Roman numerals (IV) is pronounced "ivy". Division command therefore chose the ivy leaf as the unit's emblem.

Location: stretch of beach lying in front of the town of La Madeleine

Beach sectors: Tare, Uncle

Time of landing: 6.30am

Force U, Task Force 125, commanded by Rear Admiral Moon

Units concerned:
- 4th Infantry Division
- 90th Infantry Division
- 79th Infantry Division
- 9th Infantry Division

Number of men who landed on 6 June 1944: 23,250
Equipment: 1,700 vehicles and 1,695 tons of supplies

Tare Sector
- 1st Battalion 8th Infantry Regiment
- 3rd Battalion 22nd Infantry Regiment

Sector Uncle
- 2nd Battalion 8th Infantry Regiment
- 3rd Battalion 8th Infantry Regiment

All sectors
- 8th RCT, 22nd RCT, 12th RCT
- 6th Armored Division Group
- 1st Engineer Special Brigade
- 359th RCT (90th Division)
- 327th GIR (101st Division)
- 4th Division Group
- 358th RCT
- 357th RCT
- 90th Division Group
- VIIth Corps

SERGEANT FROM THE 1ST US DIVISION

This soldier was among the first units to land on Omaha Beach. He is wearing an HBT jacket and is armed with a 30-06 calibre M1 Garand semi-automatic rifle designed to take 8-cartridge magazines which were automatically ejected when the 8th cartridge was fired. The general purpose bag, on his right leg, enabled him to carry large quantities of ammunition and explosives. In addition to his M-1923 cartridge belt, which could hold ten 8-cartridge magazines, the sergeant is also carrying a cloth bandoleer around his neck with extra ammunition. The small pouch near his right hand contains his first aid kit. He has already removed his life jacket.

D / 6.35am

The first units from the 1st US Infantry Division land on Omaha Beach

The first wave of assault comprised 8 infantry companies which should have been backed up by 29 amphibious Sherman Duplex Drive tanks from the 741st Tank Battalion. However, all but two of these tanks sank in rough seas as they were dropped too far from the coast. The A Company of the 116th Infantry Regiment came face to face with unbelievably heavy enemy fire and the men, equipment and vehicles came to a halt at the foot of the mound of pebbles stretching the length of the beach and were unable to react. The second wave of assault gathered behind the first. At 8am the situation seemed so desperate that Allied High Command considered ordering a withdrawal of troops from Omaha beach or "Bloody Omaha" as it was known by the soldiers. Meanwhile there were developments back on the beach.

All personnel involved in the Landing operations were issued with an M-1926 rubber life belt. The two tubes were inflated immediately by two pressurised gas cartridges. Large quantities of life belts were also distributed to make equipment and weapons more buoyant.

Beach sectors:
Dog Green, Dog White, Dog Red, Easy Green, Easy Red, Fox Green, Fox Red.
Pointe du Hoc: Charlie
Time of landing: 6.30am
Force O, Task Force 124, commanded by Rear Admiral Hall
Units concerned:
- 1st Infantry Division
- 29th Infantry Division
- 2nd Infantry Division

Number of men who landed on 6 June 1944: 34,250

Pointe du Hoc
- Ranger Group

Charlie Sector
- 1st Battalion 116th Infantry Regiment
- 3rd Battalion 116th Infantry Regiment
- 116th RCT (29th Division)

Dog Sector
- 2nd Battalion 116th Infantry Regiment
- 3rd Battalion 116th Infantry Regiment
- 116th RCT (29th Division)

Easy Sector
- 2nd Battalion 16th Infantry Regiment
- 16th RCT

Fox Sector
- 3rd Battalion 16th Infantry Regiment
- 1st Battalion 16th Infantry Regiment
- 18th RCT

All sectors
- 3rd Armored Division Group
- 5th & 6th Engineer Special Brigades
- 1st Division Group
- 26th RCT, 115th RCT & 175th RCT
- 29th Division Group

INFANTRY UNIT MEDIC

This soldier is carrying equipment specific to his duties over his one-piece HBT suit. Specially-designed sling attachments were used to carry first aid supply bags and there are two first aid pouches on his belt. He is wearing water-proof rubber over boots and there is a folding stretcher and first aid case by his feet.

UNDER THE PROTECTION OF A RED CROSS...

The red cross symbol was worn by all medics who were consequently protected by the Geneva conventions. For this neutrality to be granted, the red cross wearer had to be completely unarmed. Why a red cross? Because the creator of the organisation, Henri Dunant, was Swiss. While looking for an easily-identifiable symbol of neutrality he thought of his own country's flag – a white cross on a red background – and inversed the image to get a red cross on a white background.

Two elite divisions...

Omaha was the most well-defended sector on the strip of coastline that was to be the setting for the Landings. The Americans knew that the outcome of Operation Overload could be decided here and so they called in two highly-trained units. But while the 1st Infantry Division, the "Big Red One", had carved out a strong reputation for itself over two years following campaigns in North Africa and Sicily, the 29th Infantry Division had no fighting experience at all.

Big Red One Assault Museum collection, Colleville-sur-Mer

Small groups, led by determined officers, left the pebble banks, reached the dunes, attacked the bunkers and destroyed the obstacles. The 18th Infantry Regiment seized the E-1 draw enabling the troops on the beach to advance. But the meeting with the British at Port-en-Bessin did not take place and only 100 of the 2,500 tons of supplies left the beach. The Americans lost 3,880 men in one day – almost 10% of the troops who landed on 6 June 1944.

1st DIVISION

This badge is made up of a brown shield featuring a big, red number 1. The 1st Division was nicknamed "Big Red One" after the First World War, as in 1917 it became the first American division to fight alongside the Allies.

Meanwhile at Pointe du Hoc...

...men from the 2nd Rangers Battalion, under the orders of Lt. Col. James Rudder, launched an attack on the Pointe du Hoc – a steep headland lying between Omaha and Utah beach which the Germans had turned into a stronghold armed with six 155mm guns. The rangers received the order to scale the cliffs and silence the guns. Using grapnels, rope ladders and firemen's ladders mounted on DUKW amphibious vehicles, they reached the top only to find the bunkers empty – the dangerous guns had been moved inland. Surrounded by a German counter-attack, they held out several days before being joined by their comrades who had landed on the beaches.

29th DIVISION

Although it resembles the yin and yang symbol of harmony, this is in fact the symbol of the two States which made up the majority of this unit – Virginia and Maryland. These two States fought against each other during the American Civil War and the colours of the uniform can be found in the badge – blue for the Union and grey for the Confederacy. The badge represents the sacred union between these two States.

A silent army…

This is probably what surprised the opposing forces and liberated people the most, as they were used to hobnailed boots which provided the rhythm for military marches but at the same time were not very discreet. The GIs wore superb fawn-coloured, fur skin leather Uncle Sam boots and their high quality showed that the US had plenty of money and wanted the best for their soldiers.

ENGINEER SPECIAL BRIGADE : SAPPERS AND MINE CLEARERS...

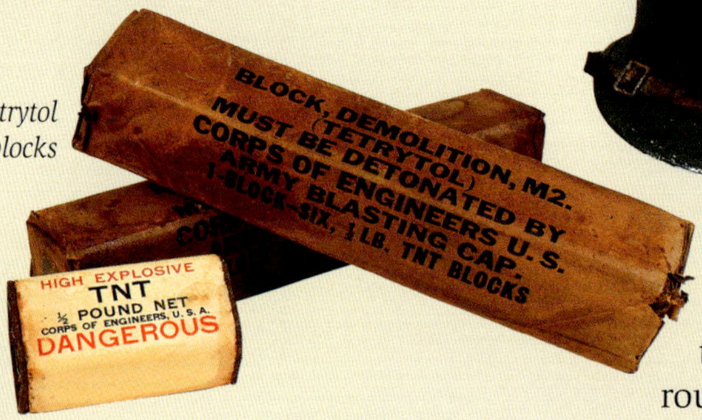

TNT stick and tetrytol demolition blocks

Big Red One Assault Museum collection, Colleville-sur-Mer.

To clear the beaches of obstacles, destroy the anti-tank walls and clear the surrounding land of mines, the Americans sent Engineer Special Brigades in the first waves of attack. They could be identified by the broad, white semi-circle painted on their helmet. When they landed on Omaha Beach, however, they were met with scenes of chaos and, caught in the fire of men from the German 352nd Infantry Division, they had no choice but to temporarily abandon their demolition mission and fight alongside their infantry comrades. These specialist units were among those who suffered the most during the Landings.

These rolls of white tape were used by American Engineer Sappers to indicate the sectors that had been cleared of mines. The tape was also used to mark out roads and cliff edges, and isolate suspect objects or equipment. The Germans used small flags with a skull and crossbones to indicate places where mines had been found.

GI LANDING EQUIPMENT

1 – Garand M1 semi-automatic rifle
2 – M-1923 cartridge belt
3 – M-1928 haversack
4 – M-1910 water bottle and cover
5 – M1 bayonet
6 – M-1924 first aid pouch
7 – M-1910 entrenching tool
8 – Mess tin cover
9 – Mess tin and cutlery
10 – M1 helmet

GI kit

The M-1928 Haversack was made up of two parts – the top part which was carried by the soldier regardless of the situation, and the bottom part which was left behind and returned to the soldier during his rest periods. During the Landings, the soldier carried the following in his haversack – mess tin, knife, spoon, fork, 4 containers of canned heat, 2 handkerchiefs, 1 box of insecticide powder, 1 bottle of water purifying tablets, 1 waterproof coat, 4 pairs of socks, a toiletry bag and a waffle-weave towel.
The lower part, which was left behind and brought later by truck, contained 1 two-piece battledress uniform, 1 vest, 1 pair of short cotton boxer shorts, 2 handkerchiefs, 1 bath towel, 2 pairs of woollen socks, 1 spare pair of boots, 2 blankets and 1 half shelter with pegs, guy ropes and pole.

SPECIAL LANDING EQUIPMENT

Besides their regulation equipment, GIs were issued with additional equipment especially for the Landings:

- 1 inflatable life belt
- 1 Pliofilm bag to protect the rifle
- 1 box of Dramamine travel sickness tablets and 2 paper sick bags
- 3 K rations (Breakfast, Dinner, Supper) and 3 D rations
- 7 packets of cigarettes and 7 small boxes of matches
- 7 packets of chewing gum
- 1 packet of razor blades
- 1 bottle of water purifying tablets and 1 box of anti-lice powder
- 3 condoms (prophylactic)
- 4 containers of canned heat for stove
- 4 spare pairs of socks
- 1 coated canvas waterproof

They also received an envelope containing a message from General Eisenhower and specially-printed bank notes – Invasion Money.

SERGEANT FROM THE DURHAM LIGHT INFANTRY

You immediately notice his Leather Jerkin – a leather waistcoat lined with woollen cloth – which he is wearing over his BD tunic. This sergeant is carrying a Sten Mk III sub-machine gun around his neck and is wearing a Mk II helmet with camouflage net. He also has a cotton canvas web belt and pouches attached to shoulder straps. More equipment can be seen in the back view (opposite page). He is carrying a small pack and has attached his regulation beaker to one of the straps and tucked wire cutters under the flap. To the right you can make out the M-1937 water bottle and web cover and on the left, above the tool, you can see the green canvas gas mask case. He is wearing lace-up boots and gaiters.

UNIT IDENTIFICATION

1 – Regiment shoulder badge, here the Durham Light Infantry
2 – Division insignia, here the 50th Northumbrian Infantry Division. The two red Ts stand for the Tees and Tyne rivers which flow through the county.
3 – Service stripes, here the red indicates an infantry unit (but not rifles). The two stripes in the unit's colour indicate that the soldier belonged to the 2nd Brigade.
4 – Sergeant rank.

D / 7.25am

The 50th "Northumbrian" Infantry Brigade launches an assault on Gold Beach

At 7.25am, 5 minutes earlier than planned, the British 50th (Northumbrian) Infantry Division craft, backed up by tanks from the 4th and 7th Dragoons, landed opposite King Sector which covered the towns of Ver-sur-Mer and Asnelles. The beach was quickly cleared of its obstacles by the special tanks of the Westminster Dragoons and despite the delaying tactics of the German troops, the British reached the N13 – the road linking Caen and Bayeux. The 231st Infantry Brigade reached Arromanches by late afternoon enabling the first parts of the artificial harbour to arrive in the area. At the same time, the 47 Royal Marine Commando headed west to rejoin the American troops of the 29th Infantry Division who had landed on Omaha Beach. They linked up on 8 June. At 11am, a second wave of units landed which was made up of the 151st and 56th Infantry Brigades. The latter liberated Bayeux the following morning – 7 June – while the 50th Division linked up with the Canadian 3rd Division that evening.

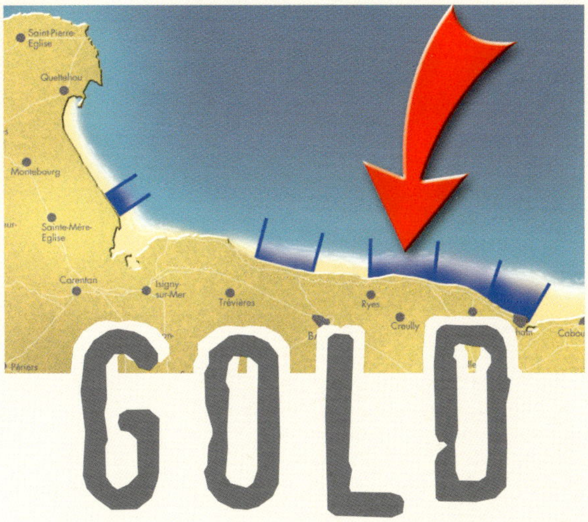

Beach sectors:
Item Green, Item Red, Jig Green, Jig Red, King Green, King Red
Maintenance and supply zone: Sun
Time of landing: 7.30am
Force G commanded by Commodore Penant
Units concerned:
- 50th (Northumbrian) Infantry Division
- 56th Brigade
- 231st Brigade
- 151st Brigade
- 89th Brigade
- 8th Armoured Brigade
- 7th Armoured Division
- 49th Infantry Division

Number of men who landed on 6 June 1944: 24,970

Item Sector
- 1st Hampshire Regiment
- 231st Brigade

Jig Sector
- 1st Dorset Regiment, 2nd Devonshire Regiment
- 47 Royal Marine Commando
- 90th and 147th Field Regiments (RA)
- 231st Brigade
- 56th Brigade

King Sector
- 6th Bn. Green Howards
- 69th Brigade

Love Sector
- 5th Bn. East Yorkshire Rgt.
- 7th Bn. Green Howards
- 86th Field Regiment (RA)
- 69th Brigade
- 151st Brigade

SOLDIER FROM THE BRITISH 3RD INFANTRY DIVISION

He is wearing a Mark III helmet, issued to 6 June 1944 assault formations, and a two-piece cotton canvas BD uniform known as Denim Overalls. He is armed with a No. 4 Mark 1 rifle and in addition to the ammunition in the pouches of his Pattern 1937 web equipment, he is carrying two canvas cartridge pouches – bandoleers – round his neck. He is holding a radio aerial case.

D / 9.30am

The BBC broadcast the first SHAEF news report: "Commanded by General Eisenhower, the Allied Naval Forces, backed up by strong Air Forces, began landing Allied troops on the northern coast of France this morning".

Helmet and insignia from the 2nd Black Watch Brigade of the 51st Highland Infantry Division. Tank aerial flag from the 2nd Brigade of the 3rd Infantry Division. The Black Watch and 3rd Armoured Brigade went on to fight alongside each other during the Battle of Caen.

D / 7.25am

Units from the 3rd Infantry Division land on Sword Beach

As scheduled, the 1st South Lancashire and 2nd East Yorkshire Regiments, backed up by tanks from the 13th and 18th Hussar Regiments, landed and immediately came under heavy fire from units of the 736th Regiment and 642nd Battalion to the east which were defending the sector. Other troops landed at the same time – Lord Lovat's Special Service Brigade, which after capturing Ouistreham, had to link up with units of the 6th Airborne Division, and the 177 Free French Commandos from the No. 4 Commando. Troops from the No. 6 Commando joined Major Howard's paratroopers at Benouville Bridge. These paratroopers had been holding the strategic point and the surrounding area since 1am. The villages of Hermanville-sur-Mer and Colleville-sur-Mer were quickly liberated but the British were prevented from advancing in the late afternoon by a counter-offensive from units of the 21st Panzer Division which were even able to reach the coast at Luc-sur-Mer and watch the Allied armada before withdrawing. The 3rd Division lost 630 men who were either injured or killed. The main objective, which involved the seizure of Caen by units of the 185th Brigade, backed up by the Staffordshire Yeomanry, was not fulfilled. Caen was not captured until 19 July.

Beach sectors:
Peter Green, Peter White, Peter Red, Queen Green, Queen White, Queen Red, Roger Green, Roger White, Roger Red.

Maintenance and supply zone:
Moon

Time of landing: 7.30am
Force S commanded by Rear Admiral Talbot

Units concerned:
- 3rd Infantry Division
- 9th Brigade
- 185th Brigade
- 8th Brigade
- 27th Armoured Brigade
- Special Service Brigade
- 51st Highland Infantry Division
- 4th Armoured Brigade

Number of men who landed on 6 June 1944: 28,845

Peter, Queen and Roger Sectors
- 1st South Lancashire Regiment
- 2nd East Yorkshire Regiment
- 1st Suffolk Regiment
- 3, 4, 6, 41, 45 Royal Marine Commandos
- 1st Special Service Brigade
- 76th Field Regiment (RA)
- 8th Brigade
- 9th Brigade, 185th Brigade
- 27th Armoured Brigade
- 3rd Division
- 4th Armoured Division
- 51st Division

D / 7.35am

The 47 Royal Marine Commando advance inland...

The young Lance Corporal on the right-hand page, who is wearing the distinctive, traditional green Royal Marine beret, belongs to the No. 4 Commando. The round insignia specific to combined operations can be seen at the top of his sleeve as can his No. 4 Commando title badge. He is wearing a Battle Jerkin over his BD uniform. The Battle Jerkin was tested out on some assault units on 6 June 1944 (see description on next page). He has regulation Pattern 37 web equipment under his Battle Jerkin (which he has not buttoned up) and you can clearly see one of the cartridge pouches. He is carrying a Wireless Set No. 38 around his waist which ensured communication between platoons and companies within a radius of 1/2 mile. He is holding an Airborne Folding Bicycle and he has slung his camouflaged Sten Mk II sub-machine gun over the handlebars. Large numbers of folding or regular bicycles were distributed to help the advancing troops reach Caen.

An "Ox and Bucks" helmet with a Fairbairn dagger and a No. 36 Mills grenade (top) and a No. 69 offensive grenade (bottom).

SAS, the parachutists in the shadows

They were the first to land on French soil to prepare for the Landings. Representing many nations, including France, they landed in the weeks leading up to 6 June 1944 to bring technical support to the Maquis. The SAS (Special Air Force) were trained fighters, and were fitted out and armed by the British. They fought alongside Resistance fighters all over the west of France and used guerrilla warfare tactics to delay German reinforcements heading north towards Normandy. The Breton Maquis are remembered for the battle in Saint-Marcel, near Malestroit, and they were among the first to lose their lives during the Landings.

THE BRITISH COMMANDO

FRENCH TROOPS IN THE NO. 4 COMMANDO UNDER KIEFFER

177 French marine riflemen joined the ranks of the British No. 4 Commando under Lieutenant Commander Philippe Kieffer. Their mission was to seize the port of Riva-Bella and link up with units from the 6th Airborne Division who jumped during the night. The men landed on Sword Beach at 7.31am. The morning of fighting in Riva-Bella saw the seizure of the casino by the Free French commandos but also claimed 41 victims.

SOLDIER FROM THE C COMPANY OF THE ROYAL REGINA RIFLES

This soldier is wearing the Battle Jerkin issued to infantrymen before the first waves of attack. Notice the double net on the helmet, the life belt around his waist and the gas mask and green canvas case around his neck. The Jerkin pockets, closed by a cord and wooden toggle system, were used to carry ammunition. He is holding an Airborne Folding Bicycle which was initially designed for airborne troops but was later issued to the second wave of troops so that they could reach Caen as quickly as possible. He is armed with a regulation No. 4 Mark I sniper rifle.

This helmet sports the emblem of the Cameron Highlanders of Ottawa, a Canadian Scottish unit which was part of the Canadian 3rd Infantry Division. The Sten Mk II sub-machine gun with skeleton stock was found at Carpiquet Aerodrome. The material badge in the foreground features the same traditional tartan.

D / 7.55am

The 3rd Canadian Infantry Division arrives on Juno Beach

The sector assigned to the 7th and 8th Brigade of the Canadian Infantry Division was located between Sword Beach and Gold Beach which were defended by the German 736th and 726th Regiments. Troops landed on Juno Beach ten minutes later than planned and the high tide, which covered part of the obstacles, resulted in many losses as the craft tried to land. After a short battle on the beach, the Canadian troops quickly advanced inland without meeting any resistance. 1,074 Canadians were put out of action following the events of 6 June 1944. Not all of the Division's objectives were accomplished, in particular Carpiquet Aerodrome was not seized and it continued to hinder advancing Anglo-Canadian troops for many weeks.

Beach sectors:
Love Green, Love Red, Mike Green, Mike Red, Nan Green, Nan White, Nan Red

Time of landing: 7.30am
Force J commanded by Commodore Oliver

Units concerned:
- 3rd Infantry Division
- 7th Brigade
- 9th Brigade
- 8th Brigade
- 2nd Armoured Brigade
- 4th Special Service Brigade

Number of men who landed on 6 June 1944: 21,400

Secteur Mike
- Royal Winnipeg Rifles
- Royal Regina Rifles
- 1st Canadian Scottish Regiment
- 12th and 13th Canadian Field Regiments (RCA)
- 7th Canadian Brigade
- 2nd Canadian Armoured Brigade
- 3rd Canadian Division

Secteur Nan
- The Queen's Own Rifle of Canada
- North Shore Regiment (New Brunswick)
- Régiment de la Chaudière
- 48 Royal Marine Commando
- 14th and 19th Canadian Field Regiments (RCA)
- 8th and 9th Canadian Brigades

1 – Rolled-up poncho
2 – Personal supplies: pullover, toiletry bag, rations and mess tin, spare clothes.
3 – Tool head
4 – Tool handle
5 – Life belt
6 – Machete scabbard

FORMAL PRUSSIAN DRESS...

If we compare two officers, two Majors for example, who fought against each other on the beaches and fields of Normandy, we can only be surprised by the noticeable differences in their uniforms. The German officer is wearing a very military-style uniform complete with rank badges, while the Allies opted for more discreet badges and less formal uniforms. It is however true that the German rank badges were

This Hauptman, or Major, is wearing a cap with white piping distinctive of the German Infantry. On his tunic he has a ribbon bar featuring the Iron Cross 2nd Class, the Winter Battle in the East Medal and the Merit Cross with Swords. He was also awarded the General Assault Badge, the Iron Cross 1st Class and the Wound Badge. His field jacket was similar to the one given to regular troops but of better quality for an officer – such jackets were issued so that officers blended in with the rest of the troops. He is carrying a pair of regulation 6 x 30 binoculars in a Bakelite case and an MP40 leather magazine pouch. He also has soft-leather officers' boots.

...OR BATTLE DRESS

much more discreet on the camouflaged smocks that they wore over their regulation uniform. With the Battle Dress, the Allies opted for a more practical and comfortable uniform. In comparison with the very formal Prussian-style German uniform, the Allies preferred a more sporty, almost relaxed, look. This was a very Anglo-Saxon approach to war which at worst was a job and at best, a sport.

This BD uniform was worn by Major Gordon Brown of the Canadian Royal Regina Rifle Regiment on Juno Beach on 6 June 1944. He was a transport officer and he landed on the beach at 11am for logistics purposes. He found a pair of German binoculars in the field which he wore on his belt throughout the battle. He kept his regulation Enfield revolver in a P38 holster that he also found. His Sten followed behind him in his Jeep. He is wearing rare assault boots and a black lanyard, specific to the Royal Regina Rifle Regiment, on his left shoulder. He also has the light blue rectangular insignia of the 3rd Infantry Division underneath the red regiment title.
The Major was awarded by the DSO – Distinguished Service Order – for the role he played in the seizure of Ardenne Abbey.

ARMOURED CORPS TANK COMMANDER

This soldier is wearing an M-1924 black milled woollen beret with the armoured unit insignia, a rubber-coated canvas-lined suit and regulation black leather laced boots. The holster for the Webley Mk IV revolver with hammer (not visible) was specific to tank crews. Attached to the M-1937 belt, it is worn low down the leg so it can be drawn from a sitting position. Notice the revolver wrist strap tied around the right epaulette. The crew member is carrying a pair of regulation 2.5 x 50 binoculars and has kept his headphones with him.

The Sherman M4 tank was used by both the American armoured units and the British and Canadian armoured corps. On the model above, the tank hull, which was initially built from welded panels, was moulded in a single piece to ensure more fluid lines and greater protection.

The Sherman tank accompanied infantry troops as they advanced across Normandy. Often loaded up with boxes, equipment, supplies and various other objects, in the eyes of the liberated people, these tanks symbolised a modern, young, fast and wealthy army.

THE ALLIED TANKS

Typically British, the Cromwell tank was used by the Armoured Reconnaissance Regiments and all the Armoured Regiments of the 7th Armoured Division. Driven by a 600hp Rolls Royce engine, it was only armed with a 75mm gun which was rather insufficient in relation to the German Tiger and Panther tanks. The British built an infantry support tank based on the Cromwell which they called the Centaur (pictured above). Driven by a 395hp Liberty engine, it was armed with a 95mm howitzer.

TANK CREW MEMBER FROM THE 1ST HUSSARS

Canadian tank crews wore the same uniforms as their British counterparts. The only difference (in keeping with tradition) was that tank crew members and some rifle regiments had black belts and straps. This soldier is wearing the 1937 BD jacket and motorcycle goggles. His revolver holster contains a GP35 automatic pistol.

SPECIAL TANKS TO GET THROUGH THE OBSTACLES

The Anglo-Canadian raid on Dieppe in 1942 demonstrated how important it was to have special tanks to break through the German defences – mine fields, anti-tank walls, etc. Colonel Hobart therefore built a whole army of tanks and "Hobart's funnies", which although eccentric in design, turned out to be very effective. In addition to the tanks shown, there were also bridge-laying tanks (to straddle the anti-tank ditches), fascine tanks (to fill in the trenches) and tanks that fired explosives into the air.

The Sherman DD Duplex Drive

The simple but clever idea was to increase the volume to mass ratio so that the tank could float. The engineer Nicolas Straussler therefore developed a system of canvas skirts mounted on moving struts and fitted with 36 inflatable chambers. The tank was powered by two small propellers driven by the tank's motor. The skirts, which were raised well up above the turret, were lowered when the tank reached land.

The Sherman Crab

The flail device, mounted on a Sherman M4A4, was a revolving drum fitted with lengths of heavy chain which sometimes had a steel ball at the end. Driven by the tank's motor, the drum turned very quickly and the chains lashed at the ground to explode buried mines. As it advanced, the tank left two lines of white chalk behind it to indicate the areas that had been cleared of mines.

The Churchill Crocodile

The flame-throwing version of the Churchill VII. The tank's turret featured a device for firing flammable liquid into the air using pressurised nitrogen. The liquid was carried in a special 400 gallon armoured trailer towed behind the tank.

SHERMAN M4 A1

Length: 20ft. / Width: 9ft.
Height: 9ft. / Weight: 30 tons
Max. speed: 24mph
Cruising range: 149 miles
Cross-country range: 100 miles
Armour plating on hull front: 76mm (3 inches)
Engine: Continental or Wright
Model: R975, 9-cylinder radial
Displacement: 15,800cc
Horsepower: 390hp at 2,400rpm
One 75mm M3 gun
One 30-calibre machine gun
One 50-calibre machine gun
Crew: 5 men
No. of models manufactured: 49,230

DESTROYER M 10

Length: 19ft. / Width: 10ft.
Height: 8ft. / Weight: 27 tons
Max. speed: 30mph
Cruising range: 199 miles
Cross-country range: 130 miles
Armour plating on hull front: 51mm
Engine: General Motors
Model: 2 x 6 cylinder 60-46-71
Displacement: 2 x 7,000cc
Horsepower: 375hp at 2,100rpm
One 76mm gun
One 30-calibre machine gun
One 50-calibre machine gun
Crew: 5 men

Sherman Firefly

The Sherman M4 75mm 113 gun lacked punch so the British replaced it with a 17-pounder 76.2mm gun which was much more hard-hitting thanks to the length of its barrel and power of its projectile. The crews camouflaged the long barrel with paint as the Germans soon picked out these "tank destroyers".

Any tank that became isolated was soon lost as without logistic support, a repair unit or tow truck, tanks soon went out of action. To tow tanks of over 30 tons, the American armoured units used powerful vehicles such as the Pacific car and Foundry M26 tank recovery tractor driven by a Hall Scott 18,000cc displacement engine which did less than 3 miles to the gallon.

NON-COMMISSIONED OFFICER FROM THE 6TH PARACHUTE REGIMENT

This "Feldwebel" (warrant officer) from the 6th Fallschirmjäger Regiment is wearing a jump smock or "bone bag" over his uniform. The only insignia on the smock is that of the Luftwaffe - paratrooper units belonged to this branch of the German Armed Forces. The collar rank patches (here yellow to indicate a paratrooper) feature the three wings of the Feldwebel rank. He is wearing a blue-grey Einheitsmütze cap which also features an eagle in flight – the symbol of the German Air Force. His helmet is clipped to his belt along with his water bottle, P08 holster and canvas MP40 sub-machine gun magazine pouch. He is holding gauntlets and is wearing high, lace-up boots which acted as jump boots.

PARATROOPERS ON FOOT?

German paratroopers had their moment of glory during the operation in Crete when they jumped one last time as part of a large airborne operation. Changes in war tactics meant that they gradually became regular troops and fought in campaigns in the Balkans, the Ukraine and Italy. The Green Devils from the 6th Paratrooper Regiment under Colonel von der Heydte fought like demons throughout the Battle of Normandy. A paratrooper regiment was initially made up of three paratrooper "hunter" regiments, an artillery regiment, an armoured corps, an anti-aircraft armoured corps, a pioneer battalion and a signals corps.

THE GREEN DEVILS

Confronted with the American paratroopers, the Germans immediately informed Colonel von der Heydte's 6th Regiment (part of the 5th Paratrooper Division) which counter attacked and succeeded in blocking off the Carentan road. One of its battalions even managed to reach Turqueville, near Saint-Mère-Eglise. On 8 June, the 6th Regiment was joined by units from the 3rd Paratrooper Division which had made their way over from Brest and were stationed in Saint-Lô. After weeks of heavy fighting, it was the men of this division who ended up trapped in the Falaise Pocket on the 19 August.

Paratrooper helmet, airborne troop gas mask bag, knife with retractable/removable blade and paratrooper badge. The dog tag is marked "6th Company of the 2nd Regiment".

The first paratrooper helmets were cut down from the standard Wehrmacht helmets.

This camouflaged tunic was issued to Luftwaffe troops fighting on the ground. The helmet is in Luftwaffe blue and features the German Air Force eagle. There is also a canvas MP40 magazine pouch and an additional canvas cartridge pouch for the Mauser 98K rifle.

Containers were also dropped with the paratroopers and once on the ground they were used as trailers to carry weapons and ammunition. This container was found in Houesville (Manche).

A REPUTATION FORGED IN CRETE

On 25 April 1941, Hitler decided to invade Crete where over 45,000 British and Greek troops had gathered. Generals von Richtofen from the Luftwaffe and Student from the Airborne troops divided their men into three units which went on to operate in different areas on the island. On 21 May, Ju 52 planes dropped the paratroopers who met with tragedy before advancing towards the British and New Zealand troops. The capture of the aerodrome proved to be a decisive factor following the arrival of heavy equipment. A week later, the Allied troops evacuated the island to flee the German onslaught. General Student's Green Devils had triumphed.

Musée Remember collection, Dinan

German paratrooper helmet, regulation folding knife and reinforced kneepads. Paratrooper helmets were initially just cut down from the 1935 model. A specific helmet was not designed or manufactured until 1938 and was originally painted blue-grey but later appeared in green-grey. The transfers were identical to those used on the general Luftwaffe model.

SERGEANT PILOT FROM THE ROYAL CANADIAN AIR FORCE

This pilot is wearing his compass on the left and map on the right (as they still do today). His equipment dates from the period between 6 and 27 June 1944. Indeed, he is still wearing the Mae West inflatable life jacket around his neck. From 27 June onwards Allied pilots no longer needed to cross the Channel to reach their aerodrome as they could operate directly from Normandy. The pilot has tied a non-regulation silk scarf around his neck to prevent his leather jacket from irritating his skin.

MASTERING THE SKIES

On 6 June 1944, the Allied Air Force made 10,536 flights, 5,809 of which were to drop 10,395 tons of bombs on systems of defence and German troops on the move. They used 1,750 planes for the operation including 900 gliders.

If the pilot was shot down, he took several items with him to help him in his escape – a map of France printed on silk that he wore around his neck for information on roads, railways, crossing points, etc., a small file to saw through bars and a compass no bigger than a penny.

HAWKER TYPOON 1-B

Wingspan: 46ft.
Length: 32ft.
Take off weight: 7 tons
Engine: Napier Sabre
Model: H-configured 24-cylinder II B
Horsepower: 2,200hp at 2,700rpm
Speed: 435mph
Ceiling: 40,000ft.
Range: 620 miles
Weapons: four 20mm Hispano guns, eight 3-inch rockets (66lb.) or two 550lb. bombs.

SPITFIRE MARK IX

Wingspan: 37ft.
Length: 31ft.
Take off weight: 3.4 tons
Engine: Merlin
Model: 61/63/66(LF)/70(HF)
Horsepower: 1,660hp
Speed: 408mph
Ceiling: 43,000ft.
Range: 435 miles
Weapons: two 20mm guns, two 50-calibre machine guns, two 550lb bombs or one 1,300lb bomb

PILOT LIEUTENANT FROM THE LUFTWAFFE

The yellow gold collar patch insignia indicate flight personnel and the rank of "Leutnent". He is wearing a "Schirmütze" – an officers' cap with the eagle specific to the Luftwaffe and is sporting the Pilot Badge next to the Parachutist Badge on the left breast of his jacket. He is carrying his flying helmet with special protective goggles. He has black leather flying boots tightened by buckles and is wearing the M-1935 air force uniform with a red-brown leather belt specific to the service. During the flight he wore a black or fawn coloured leather jacket or a beige cotton jump suit.

M-1943 cap

AN UNPRECEDENTED STRUGGLE...

Faced with this flood of several thousand aircraft, the Luftwaffe only had a few planes with which to fight back. All in all, the Luftwaffe were only able to make 319 flights – a drop in the ocean! They only had about a hundred fighters available and 55 reserve aircraft. The Allies really did have complete control of the Normandy skies.

An "Unterfeldwebel" or Sergeant's tunic. This one belonged to a member of the flight personnel and there is a 1st Class Chevron on the sleeve.

During the summer, Luftwaffe personnel wore white caps. Here, the dagger, caps, chest eagle and shoulder straps of an Oberleutnant.

ARTILLERYMAN FROM A FLAK REGIMENT

He is armed with a 98K Mauser and has an offensive grenade attached to his belt which also features two six-compartment cartridge pouches for 98K speed load magazines. He is wearing a camouflaged smock and his helmet sports the eagle specific to the Luftwaffe. As for his rank, he has white wings on red collar patches indicating an artilleryman from the Flak – the anti-aircraft artillery.

A German box for transporting 20mm Flak shells. The half-moon shaped magazine held up to twenty shells. Artillerymen alternated between a series of six powerful shells and explosives, and tracer shells used to view the flight path of the projectile and, if necessary, correct it. Here, the magazine is loaded with powerful shells. Left, a tracer shell.

A HAUPTMAN FROM THE FLAK

"FLUGZEUG ABWEHR KANONE"

This major from the anti-aircraft artillery is wearing a French military shirt under his woollen cloth uniform. Both his belt and Walther P38 pistol holster are made from the red brown leather specific to officers from the Luftwaffe. He is carrying a regulation binocular case round his neck and a small red brown leather map case on his side. The red collar patches featuring his rank indicate an artillery or anti-aircraft unit.

THE FLAK

The Flak – the German anti-aircraft artillery – was at the forefront of the Allied attack. The Flakkorps III under General Pickert suffered heavy losses in hopeless battles which saw them withdraw right back to the river Seine. The division did however bring down 26 enemy aircraft and it also destroyed over a hundred tanks, set alight by the impressive 88mm Flak 18 and 41 guns. The Flak was also equipped with 37mm and 20mm guns, including the famous 2cm Vierlingsflak whose four barrels could fire 800 to 1,800 shells a minute!

THE AMERICAN HELMET

Some units painted specific symbols on their helmets for identification purposes. This helmet belonged to the 327th Glider Infantry Regiment of the 101st Airborne Division.

On 9 June 1941, the United States decided to replace their M-1917 A1 helmet – almost identical to the British "Brodie" – with the revolutionary M1 Steel Helmet. Its originality stemmed from its double helmet design. The heavy carbon-manganese steel helmet with its main chin strap had a light vulcanised fibre liner on the inside. The two parts were completely interchangeable and the liner could be adjusted to fit any head. The helmet was painted olive-drab all over.

The originality of the helmet issued to the US army lay in its double shell. The steel helmet had a lighter fibre liner with adjustable straps and chin straps to keep the helmet in place.

Officers wore their rank insignia on the front of their helmets. Sometimes paint was used and other times a shoulder strap was welded on, as is the case here with this helmet belonging to a Lieutenant Colonel of the 90th Infantry Division, the Tough Ombres.

To be easily identified by their men, officers had a vertical white strip at the back of their helmet. NCOs had a horizontal strip.

ANGLO-CANADIAN HELMET

There were two types of helmet which succeeded each other during the conflict. The Mark II retained the lines of the helmet worn by the British during the First World War. The leather chin strap was slowly replaced by a spring-type canvas or an elasticated material version but the helmet itself did not change. The Mark III had a much more modern, flared shape hence its nickname "Turtle shell". The chin strap and fastenings were identical to the Mark II.

The Mark III helmet was much more modern in design – a far cry from the unusual form of the British "Brodie".

Resting on a jerry can used to cool the Vickers .303 machine gun, this Canadian Scottish helmet carries the traditional old insignia dating from 1914. In the foreground on the left, the old insignia and on the right, the 1944 model.

Camouflage nets sometimes concealed the division insignia.

THE GERMAN HELMET

M-1935 helmet. The yellow gold eagle transfer on the left side of the helmet was specific to the Kriegsmarine.

This is a 1942 model of the Waffen-SS helmet. It can be easily recognised as the edges have not been turned up to save time and material.

The 1935 model helmet was based on the 1915 "Stahlhelm" helmet. Its very unusual, protective shape was redesigned but its weight (2.8lb) remained the same. It was stamped in one piece from a sheet of nickel-chromium steel and was initially painted matt grey. Conditions, however, meant that it was quickly painted different shades, often according to the service (blue-grey for the Luftwaffe for example), and camouflaged with many different colours in Normandy. The liner was made up of a leather panel with several adjustable flaps and was mounted on a leather frame.

To improve camouflage, the Germans attached leafy branches to the top of their helmets used canvas, leather or rubber strap systems.

PARATROOPER HELMETS

United States

The M1C helmet was based on the standard helmet and the shell and vulcanised fibre liner were retained. In fact the M1C could only be distinguished by its special V-shape chin strap and stamped leather chin piece lined with chamois leather. The liner comprised a canvas frame and an adjustable leather headband.

This helmet, found in the Manche, belonged to Major Van Gorder, one of three surgeons from the 326th Medical Company of the 101st Airborne Division. The doctor lost his helmet at the Château de la Colombière – the site of the division's first campaign hospital. The white cross on the side was the company's emblem. The straps on the inside of the liner were practically identical to the ones found on a standard helmet.

This helmet, sporting the colours of the "Ox and Bucks" and marked "Private G. Ryder" on the inside, was found in Ranville.

Canada-Great Britain

The Airborne troop steel helmet was issued to all airborne and glider units. The chin strap, initially made of leather and later of web canvas, was adjusted and tightened using loops. The liner, attached to the shell by a nut, was identical to the one fitted in infantry helmets and featured foam pads in the upper part to absorb shocks.

Germany

The M-1938 paratrooper steel helmet. The helmet features a fawn-coloured leather liner with twelve ventilation holes, which was attached to a circular aluminium frame. Foam pads acted as shock absorbers. The double leather chin strap, attached to the shell by four rivets, could be adjusted using two press studs. The first paratrooper helmets were simply cut down from the standard M-1935 steel helmet.

INDIVIDUAL GERMAN WEAPONS

On the German side, two handguns took pride of place. The Luger Parabellum P08 automatic pistol was widely used. It made a name for itself during World War II and is still reputed even today. More modern in design and more reliable, the P38 pistol, designed by Walther, did however gain ground.

LUGER PARABELLUM P08

Length: 8.7 inches
Weight: 1.9lbs
Barrel: 4 inches
Calibre: 9mm (.35)
Rifling: 6 grooves, RH
Magazine capacity: 8
Initial velocity: 384 yards/s
Sight: fixed

WALTHER P38 PISTOL

Length: 8.5 inches
Weight: 2.1lbs
Barrel: 5 inches
Calibre: 9mm (.35)
Rifling: 6 grooves, RH
Magazine capacity: 8
Initial velocity: 384 yards/s
Sight: fixed

Grenades

German troops used two types of grenade. The offensive type, represented by the "egg", and the defensive grenade, represented by the stick grenade nicknamed "potato masher " by the soldiers. Both were triggered by a friction fuse and soldiers simply pulled on a string with a ceramic ball at the end.

INDIVIDUAL ALLIED WEAPONS

Regardless of nationality, a soldier's most faithful companion was undoubtedly his rifle. Chosen by the Supply Corps from 1936 onwards, the Garand M1 was the only semi-automatic rifle to be issued regularly. Very solid and gas-operated, it was fed by an ejectable sheet metal magazine clip loaded with eight .30 calibre cartridges. Each 12-man American fighter group was armed with 10 Garand rifles and these powerful, automatic weapons gave an undeniable advantage in the field. General Patton said that it was "the best weapon of war ever manufactured". In 1942, the British and Canadians adopted the .303 No.4 Mk 1 infantry rifle. Like its German rival (the 98K Mauser) it was a manually loaded bolt rifle and it was fed by two, 5-cartridge speed load clips inserted into the magazine under the breech. The M1 carbine was a happy compromise between the Garand rifle and the Colt .45 pistol. Although initially intended for officers, the fact that it was short, light and semi-automatic meant it soon found takers among personnel not issued with the Garand – auxiliaries, collective weapon servers, vehicle crews, etc.

GARAND M1.30 RIFLE

Length: 44 inches / Weight: 9.6lbs
Barrel: 24 inches / Calibre: .30
Rifling: 4 grooves, RH
Operation: gas-operated
Ammo feed: 8-cartridge clip
Initial velocity: 932 yards/s
Effective range: 1,199 yards

NO. 4 MK1 RIFLE

Length: 44 inches / Weight: 9lbs
Barrel: 25 inches / Calibre: .303
Rifling: 5 grooves, LH
Operation: repeating
Ammo feed: 10-cartridge magazine
Initial velocity: 812 yards/s
Effective range: 1,300 yards

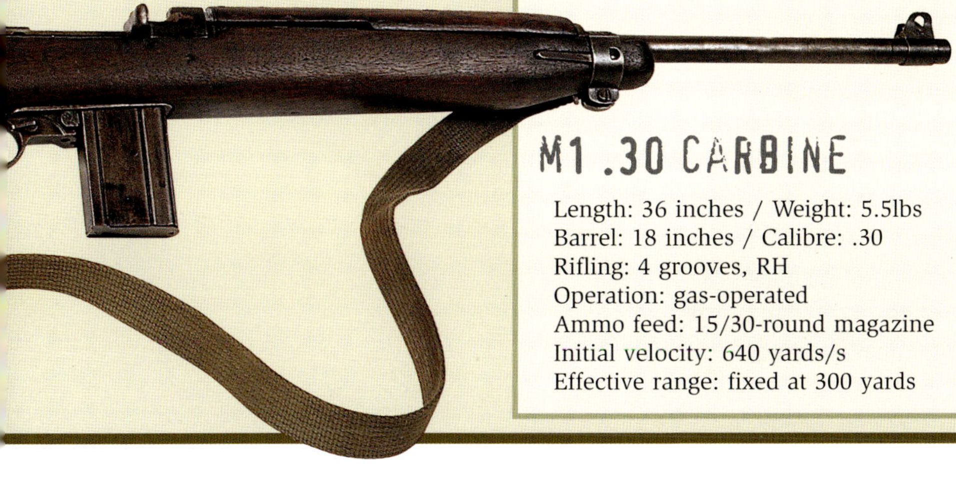

M1 .30 CARBINE

Length: 36 inches / Weight: 5.5lbs
Barrel: 18 inches / Calibre: .30
Rifling: 4 grooves, RH
Operation: gas-operated
Ammo feed: 15/30-round magazine
Initial velocity: 640 yards/s
Effective range: fixed at 300 yards

INDIVIDUAL GERMAN WEAPONS

All German soldiers were issued with a 98K Mauser – a safe, reliable, continually improved and easy-to-use weapon. The only drawback was, like nearly all weapons of the time, it had to be reloaded manually. The Reich therefore decided to issue its less sturdy and harder-to-come-by automatic or semi-automatic rifles intended for elite troops such as the paratroopers.

MAUSER 98 RIFLE

Length: 49 inches / Weight: 9lbs
Barrel: 29 inches / Calibre: 7.92mm (.31)
Rifling: 4 grooves, RH
Operation: repeating
Ammo feed: 5-cartridge magazine
Initial velocity: 951 yards/s
Effective range: 2,187 yards

WALTHER G-41 RIFLE

Length: 44 inches / Weight: 11lbs
Barrel: 21 inches / Calibre: 7.92mm (.31)
Rifling: 4 grooves, RH
Operation: gas-operated
Ammo feed: 10-round magazine
Initial velocity: 849 yards/s
Effective range: 1,312 yards

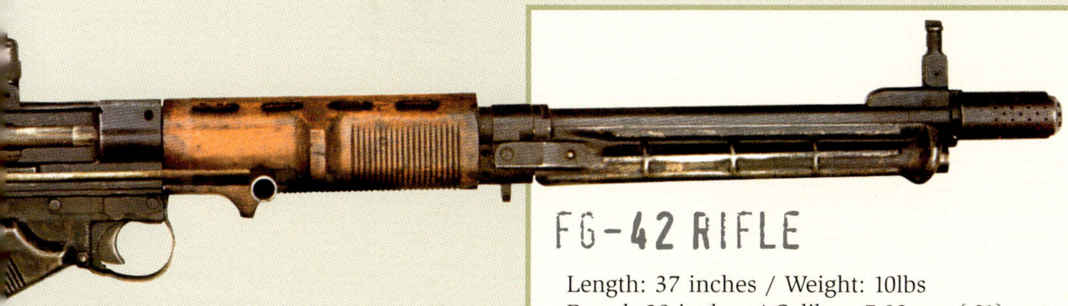

FG-42 RIFLE

Length: 37 inches / Weight: 10lbs
Barrel: 20 inches / Calibre: 7.92mm (.31)
Rifling: 4 grooves, RH
Operation: gas-operated
Ammo feed: 20-round magazine
Initial velocity: 833 yards/s
Effective range: 1,312 yards

INDIVIDUAL ALLIED WEAPONS

COLT MODEL 1911 A1 PISTOL

Length: 8.5 inches
Weight: 2.4lbs
Barrel: 5 inches
Calibre: .45
Rifling: 6 grooves, LH
Ammo feed: 7-cartridge magazine
Initial velocity: 287 yards/s
Effective range: fixed

ENFIELD NO. 2 MARK 1 REVOLVER

Length: 10.2 inches
Weight:1.7lbs
Barrel: 5 inches
Calibre: .38
Rifling: 7 grooves, RH
Magazine capacity: 7
Initial velocity: 217 yards/s
Effective range: fixed

American troops were issued with one of two handguns – either the .38 calibre Smith & Wesson revolver or the .45 calibre Colt M-1911 A1 pistol. Designed back in 1911, the Colt pistol had an exceptional service life. Using the same ammunition as the Thomson sub-machine gun, the .45 Colt turned out to be the most reliable weapon in its class. Widely considered as a prestigious weapon, it was often carried in a fawn-coloured, leather holster strapped to the thigh. The British preferred the .38 calibre Enfield No.2 Mk1 revolver.

The British Sten sub-machine gun really was a weapon from the industrial era. Largely made up of stamped and welded parts, it was easy to manufacture in large quantities and did not require complex equipment or highly-trained workers. Large quantities were shipped to British and Canadian units and it was a favourite with commandos and Resistance fighters. Although there was nothing innovative about its design, the Thompson M1-A1 was an unfailing weapon

Grenades

The Mills No.36 defensive grenade was issued to all British and Canadian units. Many were parachuted to the Resistance fighters. There was also a Mills No. 69 offensive grenade. GIs, however, preferred the US Mk 2 fragmentation defensive grenade.

featuring an unequalled safety catch and tried and tested reliability. It was gradually replaced during the conflict by the fully metal M3 which did not really go down well with the troops. Although lighter and easier to handle, its users did not like its shape and nicknamed it the "Grease Pump".

STEN MARK III SUB-MACHINE GUN

Length: 30 inches / Weight: 6.6lbs
Barrel: 7.8 inches / Calibre: 9mm (.35)
Rifling: 6.2 grooves, RH
Ammo feed: 32-cartridge magazine
Rate of fire: 550rpm
Initial velocity: 399 yards/s
Effective range: fixed

M3 SUB-MACHINE GUN

Length: 30 inches / Weight: 8.2lbs
Barrel: 8 inches / Calibre: .45
Rifling: 4 grooves, RH
Ammo feed: 30-cartridge magazine
Rate of fire: 400rpm
Initial velocity: 306 yards/s
Effective range: fixed

THOMSON M1-A1 SUB-MACHINE GUN

Length: 32 inches / Weight: 10.5lbs
Barrel: 10.5 inches / Calibre: .45
Rifling: 6 grooves, RH
Ammo feed: 20/30-cartridge magazine
Rate of fire: 700rpm
Initial velocity: 307 yards/s
Effective range: 109 yards

The MP40 sub-machine gun, created by Hugo Schmeisser, was very popular with both its legitimate owners and Allied soldiers, who seized them whenever they could.

This motorcyclist from the Luftwaffe, who can be identified by the specific eagle on his helmet and his belt buckle, is armed with a MP40 that he is carrying around his neck. The gun was fed by 32-round magazines carried in special pouches.

The MP44 "Sturmgewehr" assault rifle design was innovative for the time as it supposedly combined rifle precision with sub-machine gun firing power.
This hybrid concept produced a weapon with outstanding features for the period.

INDIVIDUAL GERMAN WEAPONS

MP40 SUB-MACHINE GUN

Length: 33 inches
Weight: 8.9lbs
Barrel: 9.9 inches
Calibre: 9mm (.35)
Rifling: 6 grooves, RH
Ammo feed: 32-round magazine
Rate of fire: 500rpm
Initial velocity: 399 yards/s
Effective range: 109 yards (total range 219 yards)

MP44 STURMGEWEHR ASSAULT RIFLE

Length: 37 inches
Weight: 11.2lbs
Barrel: 17 inches
Calibre: 7.92mm (.31)
Rifling: 4 grooves, RH
Operation: gas-fed
Ammo feed: 30-round magazine
Rate of fire: 500rpm
Initial velocity: 707 yards/s
Effective range: 875 yards

COLLECTIVE ALLIED WEAPONS

When it came to collective weapons, the Allies used the American version of the Bren (the .30 calibre Browning Automatic Rifle) and .30 and .50 calibre Browning machine guns.

VICKERS .303

Length: 43 inches
Weight (with bipod): 33lbs
Weight (with tripod): 50lbs
Barrel: 28 inches
Calibre: 7.69mm (.303)
Rifling: 4 grooves, RH

Operation: recoil
Ammo feed: canvas belt
Cooling method: water-cooled
Rate of fire: 500rpm
Initial velocity: 814 yards/s
Effective range: 3,800 yards

BREN AUTOMATIC RIFLE

Length: 45.5 inches
Weight: 22lbs
Barrel: 25 inches
Calibre: .303
Rifling: 6 grooves, RH

Operation: gas-operated
Ammo feed: 30-round magazine
Cooling method: air-cooled
Rate of fire: 500rpm
Initial velocity: 814 yards/s
Effective range: 2,000 yards

PIAT (PROJECTOR, INFANTRY, ANTI-TANK)

Length: 39 inches
Weight: 34lbs
Maximum range: 115 yards
Weight of projectile: 2.4lbs
Initial velocity: 150 yards/s

The bazooka rocket launcher, which fired hollow-charge rockets, was preferred to the more powerful yet difficult to use British PIAT.

GERMAN COLLECTIVE WEAPONS

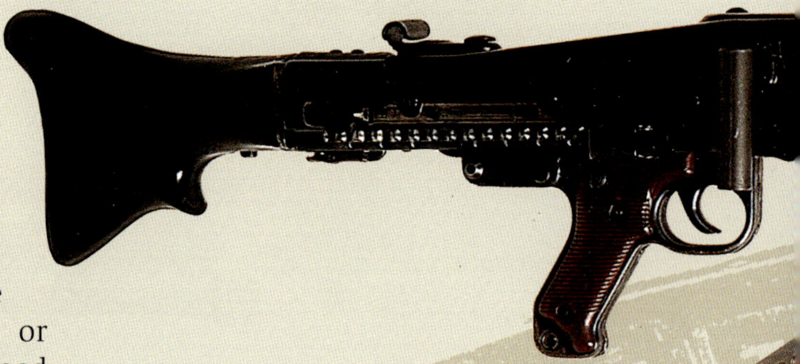

The Great War demonstrated the strategic importance of machine guns as regards saturating the battle field. But these guns were heavy and the mechanism was either too complex or not sturdy enough. They often jammed or overheated and could only be carried by soldiers if they were taken apart. Soldiers the world over dreamt of a light gun with a high firing rate which could be fired over long periods of time in complete safety and without overheating. Their dreams came true with the MG42 machine gun – an improved and more reliable version of the MG34. In its lightest bipod version, the gun could be carried by one man and used as an automatic rifle. It was fairly reliable despite an unbelievable firing rate of 1,200rpm. The overheating problem, which caused the barrel to turn red hot after continual firing, was solved by an almost immediate replacement. The operation only took a couple of seconds and no special tools were required, just asbestos gloves to protect the user from burns. The MG42 broke new ground, both as regards design and performance, and is still in use in many armies throughout the world.

The 1,200rpm firing rate of the MG42 meant that a large amount of ammunition was required which was carried in 25-round metal cases.

MG42

Length: 48 inches
Weight (with bipod): 26lbs
Weight (with tripod): 42lbs
Barrel: 21 inches
Calibre: 7.92mm (.31)
Rifling: 4 grooves, RH
Operation: recoil or gas-operated
Ammo feed: metal belt
Cooling method: air-cooled
Rate of fire: 1,100 to 1,200rpm
Initial velocity: 827 yards/s
Effective range: 2,187 yards

MG34

Length: 48 inches / Weight (with bipod): 27lbs
Weight (with tripod): 44lbs

Barrel: 25 inches
Calibre: 7.92mm (.31)
Rifling: 4 grooves, RH
Operation: short recoil
Ammo feed: metal belt or double-drum magazine
Cooling method: air-cooled
Rate of fire: 800 to 900rpm
Initial velocity: 837 yards/s
Effective range: 2,187 yards

Chief-of-the-Piece

The Chief-of-the-Piece was an infantry sergeant. Note his combination of leather and canvas MP40 magazine pouches. He is wearing an M-1943 field jacket made of woollen cloth. His special Chief-of-the-Piece equipment includes a pair of 6 x 30 binoculars and a leather map case or "Meldetasche", a folding spade with cover, a "Sturmgepäck" (combat pack) and a camouflaged, M-1942 helmet.

Gunner

This machine gunner, with the rank of "Obergefreiter" (Corporal) and the title of 1st MG gunner, is wearing a green Battle Dress uniform and a camouflaged M-1935 helmet. He is armed with a P08 pistol and a stick grenade. Note also his protective goggles with tinted glass lenses and asbestos gloves, essential for replacing the burning hot machine gun barrel, carried in a special case.

THE MG CORPS

The machine gunners corps

A corps consisted of three men. The MG42 could be operated on a bipod (LMG) or a heavy tripod with scope mount (SMG). Its very specific operating system enabled a firing rate of 1,200 rounds per minute, which meant that ammunition was rapidly used up and the weapon overheated considerably. For this reason the barrel was frequently replaced with the one in the cylindrical case shown below.

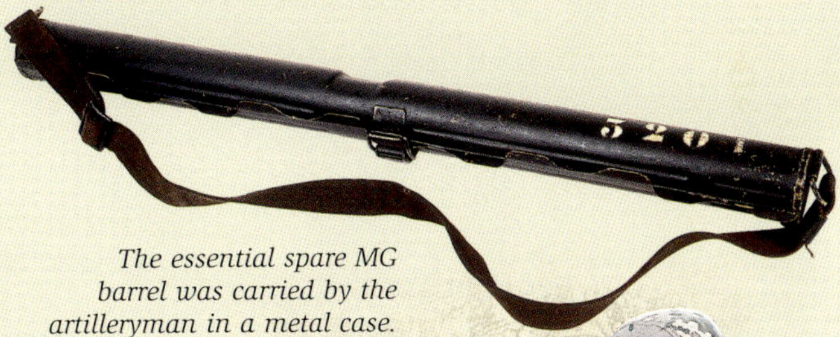

The essential spare MG barrel was carried by the artilleryman in a metal case.

Artilleryman

This soldier would have been responsible for loading the MG. He is carrying ammunition cases and a spare barrel inside its metal holster. This young artilleryman is wearing a BD field jacket with M-1936 epaulettes. He is wearing lace-up boots with canvas gaiters and a camouflaged, M-1942 helmet.

"UNTERSCHARFÜHRER" (MG GUNNER) FROM THE WAFFEN-SS

This soldier is holding the light machine gun version of the "Machinengewehr 42" with its folding bipod. He is wearing a camouflaged "Tarnjacke" smock on top of his "Feldgrau" uniform. On his right lapel you can see the SS runes and on the left lapel, the soldier's rank – here, the "Unterscharführer" or sergeant.
He has hooked his gun repair kit to his belt. The one in the photo is a late, replacement version made of cardboard. He is wearing iron-soled, lace-up boots and canvas gaiters. Metal staples have been used to attach the camouflaged canvas helmet cover to his helmet.

This compact magazine was used for MG15 machine guns mounted on aircraft or tanks. A special ammunition transport chain system moved from one case to the other by means of a spring which was wound up with a spanner.

This repair kit for both MG35 and MG42 models took up exactly the same amount of space as a standard ammunition box. It held two metal cans containing oil and petrol for cleaning the weapon. There was also a tool kit and loading belt with a special machine for restocking metal belts with cartridges.

This box-can was exactly the same shape as a standard ammunition box but contained cooling liquid for the old MG 08/15 machine gun. It was connected to a cooling mantle via a flexible pipe attached to the tap on the left. With its interesting camouflage, this rather old-fashioned piece of equipment was often used by the occupying troops patrolling the Atlantic Wall.

A gunner's kit (here, for an MG34) contained everything required to dismantle, clean and repair the weapon: an oil cloth, special dismantling spanners, a cartridge extractor, a spare breech, a priming strap and an adaptable sight for anti-aircraft combat.

The IF 8 infantry trailer could carry up to 772lbs of equipment including weapons, ammunition and supplies, etc. Mounted on tyres, it could be towed by a vehicle, horses or simply pulled by hand. In this photo, a Panzerschreck 54 is resting on the trailer.

LYING IN AMBUSH IN THE SUNKEN ROADS...

PANZERFAUST 60

Length: 31 inches
Weight: 2lbs
Calibre: 88mm (3.5 inches)
Range: 164 yards
Projectile weight: 7lbs
Penetration: 7 inches

PANZERSCHRECK 54

Length: 64 inches
Weight: 21lbs
Calibre: 88mm (3.5 inches)
Range: 164 yards
Projectile weight: 7lbs
Penetration: 3 inches

SS-PANZER GRENADIER, FLAME-THROWER CARRIER

This soldier is wearing a "pea" camouflaged BD field jacket with the distinctive Waffen-SS eagle on his left sleeve. His M-1942 helmet has a bell-shaped rim. He is carrying a "Flammenwerfer 41" flame-thrower which weighs 90lbs and contains petrol lit by a jet of hydrogen as it leaves the tube. Five squirts of liquid could thus produce temperatures of up to 800°C.

THE BATTLE OF THE HEDGEROWS

The Normandy bocage had drastic consequences for the fully mechanised Allied army and its strategies. The Allied tanks and vehicles were of little use there and the small, mobile and well-camouflaged groups, machine gunners, grenades and "Panzerfaust" often claimed the upper hand. The otherwise peaceful Normandy countryside, which was divided into thousands of plots of land enclosed by thick, virtually impenetrable hedges, turned into a battle field where death threatened to strike anywhere and at any time. The tanks, which elsewhere had been the Allies' spearhead, got stuck in the entrances to sunken lanes dotted across the bocage area. Each field and road became the subject of fierce fighting. The Allies had planned on fully liberating Brittany by D + 60, however, this was far from being the case by the end of July, and hundreds of wounded and dead, scattered across the countryside, bore witness to the intensity of the fighting.

The American offensive, which began after the capture of Cherbourg on 26 June 1944, was intended to liberate the entire Contentin area and Brittany region, however what ought to have been as easy as a walk in the park, actually turned out to be a lethal trap. Riflemen and tank crews fell into great difficulty, and losses amounted to as much as one man lost for every yard gained.

THE HEDGECUTTER FOR BREAKING THROUGH HEDGES

The impenetrable hedges, which lined the sunken lanes of the Normandy bocage, soon proved to be a major obstacle for the American tanks. The other inconvenience was that as they tried to scale the hedges, the underside of the tank (i.e. its most vulnerable part) would be exposed to the enemy. An ordinary sergeant came up with the bright idea of fitting the front of Sherman tanks with powerful metal teeth which could rip away at the hedges. There was no problem finding the raw material for making these teeth as thousands of obstacles on the beaches known as "Czech hedgehogs" were perfect for the job.

The date beneath each emblem refers to the date the unit actually engaged in combat.

BRITISH AND CANADIAN DIVISIONS IN NORMANDY

British Infantry Divisions

3rd Infantry Division
6 June

15th (Scottish) Infantry Division
14 June

43rd (Wessex) Infantry Division
24 June

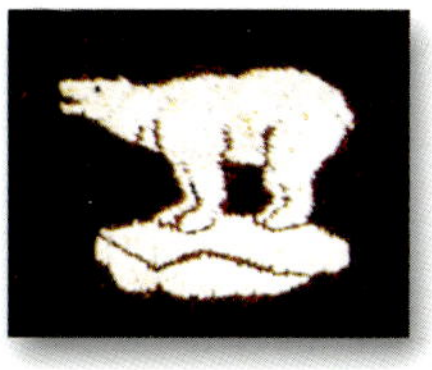

49th (West Riding) Infantry Division
12 June

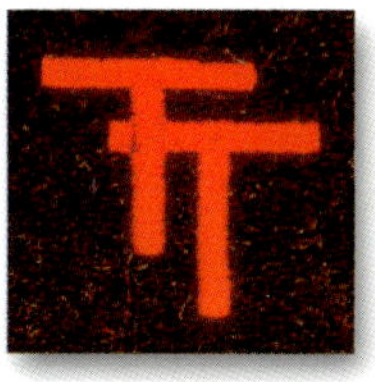

50th (Northumbrian) Infantry Division
6 June

51st (Highland) Infantry Division
7 June

53rd (Welsh) Infantry Division
27 June

59th (Staffordshire) Infantry Division
27 June

British Armoured Divisions

Guards Armoured Division
28 June

7th Armoured Division
8 June

11th Armoured Division
13 June

79th Armoured Division
6 June

Canadian Infantry Divisions

2nd Canadian Infantry Division
7 July

3rd Canadian Infantry Division
6 June

Canadian Armoured Divisions

4th Canadian Armoured Division
31 July

2nd Canadian Armoured Brigade
6 June

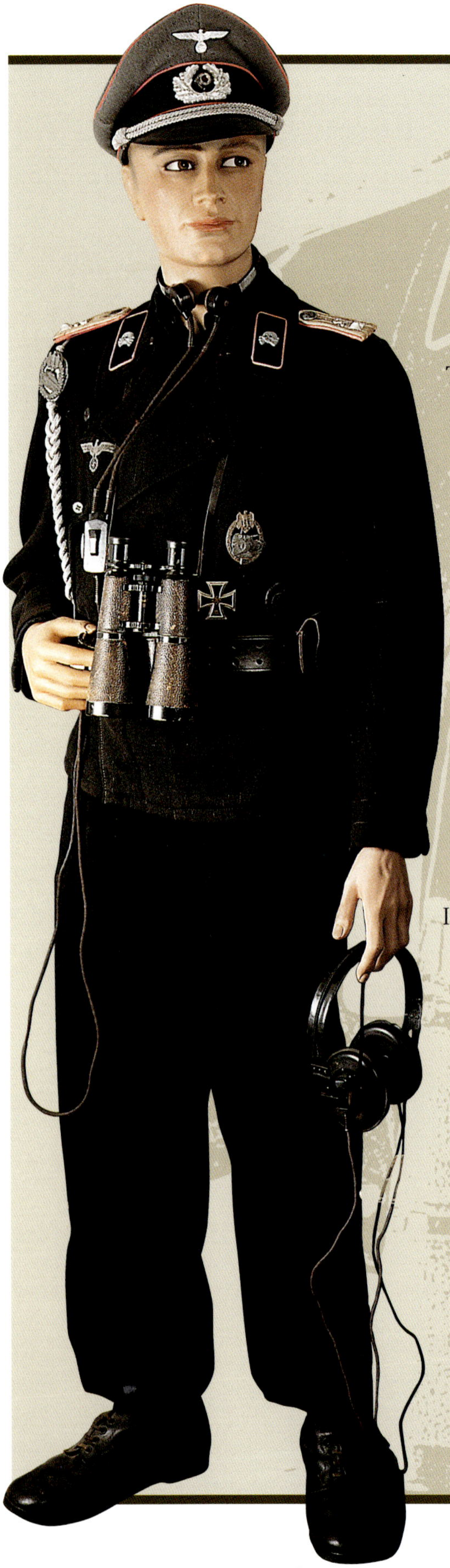

"OBERLEUTNANT" FROM THE 2ND PANZER DIVISION

This "Oberleutnant" or tank commander is wearing a black woollen cloth field jacket adopted by tank and armoured reconnaissance vehicle crews in 1934. There were no buttons or pockets to hinder his movements inside the vehicle. The black uniform was necessary inside a vehicle that tended to sweat oil, petrol and powder, and is also reminiscent of the uniforms worn by Prussian hussars, whose skull and crossbones emblem was later adopted by the Panzers. The soldier's skull and crossbone collar badges, epaulettes and cap are edged with pink piping – pink being the colour representing the German tank units. The officer is holding headphones used for radio communication inside the tank. He is also wearing a throat microphone around his neck, activated by the switch on his chest just to the left of his pair of high power binoculars. He has been decorated with the Iron Cross and the rare 25 Panzer Assault Badge.

NON-COMMISSIONED OFFICER FROM THE MOTORIZED TROOPS

This soldier is wearing a canvas raincoat with no visible rank badges, and a brown-leather Heer belt. He is armed with a Walther P38 pistol carried inside an old-style holster and is wearing an old-style field cap. This cap was not actually authorised, however many non-commissioned officers, and even officers, continued to wear it until the end of the war. Having climbed down from his vehicle, this soldier, who has tied a Normandy scarf round his neck (hardly in keeping with regulation clothing) is still wearing his headphones, which, as they were mounted on a strip of canvas, could be used while wearing a cap.

GERMAN TANKS

There's 88 and there's 88... Equal calibre does not necessarily mean exactly the same type of ammunition, as these two German 88mm shells illustrate. On the left, the impressive 88mm Pak 43 shell, fired by Tiger tanks. Its perforating head could pierce through Allied tank armour. It was a completely different size to the 88mm Flak shell shown on the right, which was used for anti-aircraft fire.

PANTHER G (SDKFZ 171)

Length: 23ft. / Width: 11ft.
Height: 10ft / Weight: 44 tons
Max. speed: 34mph
Cruising range: 124 miles
Cross-county range: 62 miles
Armour plating on hull front: 80mm at 35°
Armour plating on hull sides: 50mm at 60°
Armour plating on turret front: 100mm at 80°
Armour plating on turret sides: 45mm at 65°
Engine: Maybach HL 230 P 30
Model: V-12 cylinder / Displacement: 23,880cc
Horsepower: 700hp at 3,000 rpm
One 75mm KwK 42 L/70 gun
Two MG 34 machine guns
Crew: 5 men
No. of models manufactured: 6,000 (all types)

The Panther was unquestionably the best German tank and, undoubtedly the tank with the best armour in the Second World War. It had many strong points: well-positioned, thick armour plating, a high-performance 75mm 70-caliber gun, a relatively high speed and range, given the tank's moving mass, and good mechanical reliability.

The Tiger tank was the Allies' most feared enemy. Its 88mm gun had such powerful penetration with its velocity of 885 yards/s, that its Pak 43 shells could pierce through any known armour. This 54-ton monster was also protected by armour, which measured 4 inches at its thickest, making it virtually invincible. The tank was completely covered by a special "Zimmermit" coating which prevented it from picking up mines. 1,355 tanks of this kind were manufactured.

TIGER E (SDKFZ 181)

Length: 21ft. / Width 12ft.
Height: 10ft. / Weight: 54 tons
Max. speed: 28 miles/h
Cruising range: 121 miles
Cross-country range: 68 miles
Armour plating on hull front: 100mm at 80°
Armour plating on hull sides: 80mm at 90°
Armour plating on turret front: 100mm at 80°
Armour plating on turret sides: 80mm at 64°
Engine: Maybach HL 230 P 45
Model: V-12 cylinder / Displacement: 23,880cc
Horsepower: 700hp at 3,000rpm
One 88mm KwK 36 L/56 gun
Two MG34 machine guns
Crew: 5 men

PANZER IV H (SDKFZ 161)

Length: 19ft. / Width: 11ft.
Height: 9ft. / Weight: 25 tons
Max. speed: 24 miles/h
Cruising range: 130 miles
Cross-country range: 81 miles
Armour plating on hull front: 80mm at 80°
Armour plating on hull sides: 30mm at 90°
Armour plating on turret front: 50mm at 80°
Armour plating on turret sides: 30mm at 64°
Engine: Maybach HL 120 TRM
Model: V-12 cylinder
Displacement: 11,870cc
Horsepower: 300hp at 3,000rpm
One 75mm KwK 40 L/48 gun
Two MG34 machine guns
Crew: 5 men

The Panzer IV was the German army's most frequently used tank during the war. However its weaknesses became evident towards the end of the war as it was too slow and its armour plating was inadequate.

SS PANZER REGIMENT 2 "OBERSCHARFÜHRER"

Like the Heer tank crew, this soldier is wearing a black uniform, adopted by Waffen-SS armoured car crews in 1938 but not issued to tank crews until three years later. On his left sleeve he is wearing the SS National Eagle and the 2nd SS Panzer Division "Das Reich" armband. His collar lapels indicate that he is an "Oberscharführer" (the equivalent of a staff sergeant). He has been decorated with the Iron Cross, the Tank Assault Badge and the Imperial Wound Badge. He is wearing a pair of high-power binoculars, headphones and a radio throat microphone round his neck and is holding the power connector which connected the microphone to the tank. To protect himself, he is armed with a Walther P38 pistol hooked to his belt which features a Waffen-SS buckle.

The end of a legend

On 8 August 1944, in a field near the village of Cintheaux, Tiger tank # 007 was hit, no doubt, by a Typhoon fighter-bomber rocket. The explosion blasted the turret away killing the entire crew outright. This tank was operated by the German army's most famous tank chaser, "Hauptsturmführer" (Commander) Mickaël Wittmann, who was in charge of the "schwere SS Panzer Abteilung 101". In total, Wittmann destroyed 132 anti-tank guns and 138 tanks during his campaigns in the Balkans, Russia and France.

THE SS PANZER SPEARHEAD

The Normandy skies were free from the Luftwaffe and so the only thing the Allied units flooding into Normandy had to fear was the arrival of tanks or 'panzers'. There may not have been many of them compared to the Allied tanks, and they may have been slow to reach the battlefield, but once in place, they often took the upper hand. Alongside the Heer's armoured formations, the Panzer SS crews carved out a formidable reputation for themselves among the Allied armoured units.

Men from the Panzer SS tank units were very fond of this leather jacket from the Kriegsmachine depots which had initially been intended for submariners. Leather provided much better protection against impact and particularly against flames. The epaulettes feature the distinctive pink piping of the tank units. The picture also shows a small leather map case and a Luger P08 gun. A "Leistandarte Adolf Hitler" armband is lying on the jacket along with Waffen-SS collar patches and a Tank Assault Badge. The stamped metal skull and cross bones badge would have been worn on the cap.

UNITS FIGHTING IN THE BATTLE OF NORMANDY

For a while, Hitler believed that the Normandy Landings were just a distraction and that the Allied armies were more likely to focus on France's north coast. For this reason he only authorised SS tank units to advance slowly. Although the 12th SS Panzer Division "Hitler Youth" left Evreux on 7 June 1944 for the Normandy beaches, the 2nd SS Panzer Division "Das Reich", which was also alerted the same day, left its Toulouse base but did not arrive in the southern area of Caen until the 28 June, i.e. 22 days after the Landings.

On 11 June, the Führer, who was becoming increasingly aware of the advancing Allied troops, ordered the 1st SS Panzer Division "Liebstandarte" (stationed in Belgium), the 9th SS Panzer Division "Hohenstauffen" and the 10th SS Panzer Division "Frundsberg" (stationed in Poland) to head towards the Normandy coast. Meanwhile, men from the 17th SS Panzer Grenadier Division stationed in Poitiers, led counter attacks in the Normandy bocage.

"JABOS, JABOS!"

This is what the German soldiers (whether "Panzer grenadiers" or tank crews) would shout whenever "Jabos" or "Jagdbombengeschwader", i.e. Typhoon fighter-bombers, appeared overhead with their lethal rockets. These planes would make a low altitude reconnaissance flight followed by a second flight when they released rockets, destroying everything in their wake. The only way to escape these exterminating angels was to disappear or 'melt' into the background. The Germans had become experts in camouflaging their infantrymen, but this was not enough in itself. Vehicles and tanks also had to be transformed into moving bushes to avoid enemy fire.

MG ARTILLERYMAN FROM THE "SS PANZER-GRENADIER"

It was the artilleryman who carried the ammunition in a firing group serving an MG34 or MG42 machine gun. This soldier is wearing an M-1944 "pea" camouflaged uniform and his helmet is covered with camouflaged material. His cylindrical case is carrying a spare MG barrel. As was often seen in battle, the solder has a belt of cartridges around his neck, ready to supply the machine gun. He is armed with a 98K Mauser, a 1924 stick grenade and an "egg" grenade.

The camouflage used by the Germans during the Battle of the Hedgerows was one of the best of its kind. This helmet, with its cover made of camouflaged canvas, illustrates to what extent the German soldiers – and in particular the paratroopers and Waffen-SS soldiers – had become experts in the art of melting into the background.

All kinds of material and equipment were camouflaged, including battle dress uniforms, ammunition boxes, equipment and vehicles.

THE ART OF CAMOUFLAGE

No other army in the world developed the art of individual camouflage more than the Waffen-SS. The Wehrmacht had been using camouflaged canvas since 1925 but the SS technical offices also developed a whole range of gaudy colours, with original combinations and shades, which meant that the soldiers literally disappeared into the background. The first camouflaged cloth helmet covers appeared in 1937, followed by the first uniforms. At the end of the war, Professor Schick developed an "undergrowth" camouflage which was one of the best of its kind. Many different uniforms were developed, of which the most famous, perhaps because it was the most widely used in Normandy, was the "pea" camouflaged uniform. The Allies never used camouflaged equipment. The Americans tested it out in Normandy when they equipped certain units with camouflaged uniforms and helmet covers. However, due to the fact that these uniforms were very similar to those worn by the German army, the Americans soon abandoned the test.

Equipment camouflage also developed during the war. The traditional black became far too visible and gradually gave way to colours which blended in better with the background. Here, "Feldmütze" – the standard caps of the 12th Panzer SS Hitlerjugend regiment. On the left, the initial black woollen cloth M-1943 cap was replaced by camouflaged models with and without badges.

THE WAFFEN-SS IN THE HEAT OT THE BATTLE...

On the left, a camouflaged helmet and cap, a few badges and rank badges. From left to right, an armband from the 1st SS Panzer Division bearing the inscription "Adolf Hitler" in gothic font; some collar patches and epaulettes from the uniform of an "Unterscharführer" sergeant of the SS Panzer Grenadier, next to them a pair of epaulettes with pink piping from a uniform belonging to a "Sturmmann" from the 1st SS Panzer Division and bearing the interweaved initials "LAH", "Leibstandarte Adolf Hitler". On the far left, beneath the collar patches, the National Eagle, worn on the left arm. On the far right, a packet of bandages made especially for Waffen-SS units.

A camouflaged helmet, typical of those worn during the Battle of Normandy; a Walther PP pistol holster and a Waffen-SS officer's belt. The belt was found at the Valtontaine junction near the village of Hambie. The signpost in the background is one of many signs used by the Germans to effectively yet discretely guide their own troops. The symbols on this sign indicate a transport unit belonging to the 3rd company of the SS Panzer Division "Das Reich".

The very distinctive emblem of the SS featured two capital "S's" from the German word "Schutzstaffel" meaning "protection group". When set up in 1923, the SS was an integral part of the SA, a highly trained paramilitary organization. The SS was originally formed, firstly, to protect V.I.Ps from the N.S.D.A.P. (the Nazi party), and secondly, as a peacekeeping force. In 1933, part of this force was moved into the army and militarised before finally being named "Waffen-SS" after the Battle for Poland. The skull and crossbones on the cap was inspired by badges worn by the "Leibhusaren" or Prussian Hussars.

Cap, collar patches and shoulder straps from a Waffen-SS "Hauptsturmführer" (Captain).

This Feldmütze, worn by tank crews, is embroidered with aluminium thread piping distinguishing it from caps worn by the troops. The badges – the National Eagle and the skull and crossbones – were sewn on with aluminium thread.

Waffen-SS armoured units in Normandy

The Waffen-SS lined up the following regiments on the Normandy battlefield:

- SS-PZ.Rgt. 2 of the 2nd SS Armoured Division "Das Reich"
- SS-Pz.Rgt. 12 of the 12th SS Armoured Division "Hitlerjugend"
- SS-Pz.Rgt. 1 of the 1st SS Armoured Division "Leibstandarte SS Adolf Hitler"
- SS-Pz.Rgt. 9 of the 9th SS Armoured Division "Hohenstaufen"
- SS-Pz.Rgt. 10 of the 10th SS Armoured Division "Frundsberg"
- 101st Heavy SS Panzer Battalion

COMMANDER FROM AN SS PANZER GRENADIER COMPANY

Although this soldier was a group commander there are no markings on his uniform to show his rank. The slight camouflage on his modern helmet was interrupted on the right to reveal the SS runes. Over his uniform he is wearing a camouflaged smock, known as a "Tarnjacke", fastened with a leather lace. Note the knife in his boot, his belt buckle bearing the Waffen-SS emblem and his canvas MP40 magazine pouch. He is also equipped with a pair of regulation binoculars and has a stick grenade tucked into his belt. He is carrying the bear minimum of equipment.

MEANWHILE BACK ON THE BEACHES... THE "MULBERRIES" WERE CONSTANTLY IN ACTION...

The "Mulberries" were the Allies' spectacular answer to keeping the invading troops supplied with provisions. While waiting for a port to be seized or captured, thousands of tons of equipment and supplies needed to be docked somewhere. The Allies therefore decided to build two artificial, pre-fabricated harbours which could be entirely disassembled and which followed the invading troops across the channel. As soon as the battles were over on the beaches the two harbours were put together.

Breakwaters like a giant Meccano kit

Breakwaters were erected to protect the pier-heads from wave swells. There were three types of breakwater. A floating boom or 'bombardon', which was erected and anchored to the seabed at a depth of 10 fathoms. It could reduce swells by at least a third and enclosed an area where liberty ships dropped anchor while waiting to unload. A second "wall" of breakwaters was anchored at a depth of 16 fathoms. It was made up of Phoenix blocks – enormous, hollow, concrete caissons which had been towed across the Channel. These blocks were approximately 66 yards long, 19 yards wide, 20 yards high and weighed 7 tons. Once in place, specially designed gates were opened and the blocks sank to the bottom of the seabed. Some of these blocks were armed with 40mm anti-aircraft guns. Then, finally, the Phoenix block barrier was extended to the east side by a barrier made up of blockships which were carefully aligned before being sunk. On Mulberry A at Omaha beach, 14 blockships, known as "Corncobs", formed the sea wall leaving two 66-yard openings seaward.

Landing piers

The main problem was how to ensure that the harbour remained operational on a day-to-day basis with a 20-foot tidal amplitude. This problem was solved by Loebnitz pier-heads – enormous sliding blocks mounted on four posts anchored to the seabed – which moved with the action of the tide and swells. Positioned over half a mile out at sea, they were connected to the beach by 'Whale' roadways resting on floating 'Beetle' pontoons. Some roadways could even support the weight of 32-ton Sherman tanks! What a result!

A high-performing, ingenious system

Let's take the example of an LST (Landing Ship Tank) which could be completely unloaded in less than 40 minutes. If it had to dock on the beach, the ship would have required fourteen hours for the same unloading operation to be carried out.

The American sector. Mulberry A at Saint-Laurent-sur-Mer

The first parts arrived on 6 June 1944. The harbour was due to be completed on 27 June, but actually received its first LST on 17 June. On the 18 June, 11,000 men, 2,000 vehicles and 9,000 tons of supplies were unloaded. Four days of exceptionally stormy weather from 19 to 22 June caused extensive damage to the harbour. From then on, only Mulberry B could be used to unload supply convoys.

The British sector. Mulberry B at Arromanches-les-Bains

Work on this harbour also started on D-Day, but it took longer to build. Only 2,000 tons were unloaded on 18 June. This harbour was also damaged by the storm but valiantly fulfilled its mission regardless until Cherbourg harbour was ready to take over on 26 July.

SERGEANT FROM THE 2ND US INFANTRY DIVISION

This soldier is armed with a US M1 carbine and a canvas magazine pouch attached to the stock. This weapon had the same calibre as the M1 Garand rifle but its revolver-type ammunition was much less powerful. Short and light, it was a kind of transition weapon between the revolver and the rifle. This NCO, who is wearing a multi-purpose M-1936 musette bag on his back, is wearing an M-1941 field jacket and trousers made of mustard-coloured woollen cloth. He is carrying a map case, a pair of binoculars and a TL 122 torch which is hooked to his webbing equipment, and is wearing protective goggles round his neck.

THE US INFANTRY DIVISIONS IN NORMANDY

1st Division
"Big Red One"

2nd Division
"Indian Head"

4th Division
"Ivy"

5th Division
"Red Diamond"

8th Division
"Golden Arrow"

9th Division
"Varsity"

28th Division
"Keystone"

29th Division
"Blue and Grey"

35th Division
"Santa Fe"

79th Division
"Lorraine"

80th Division
"Blue Ridge"

83rd Division
"Ohio"

90th Division
"Tough Ombres"

Editions Hirlé Stasbourg collection

Each American division was represented by a carefully selected emblem which symbolised the unit. Made from embroidered material, these badges were sewn onto the left sleeve of the uniform, just above the rank badge. These badges were not just chosen randomly but to some extent told the unit's story. For example, the 79th Division's Lorraine-cross recalls the unit's participation in the Battle of Lorraine alongside the "poilus" (French First World War soldiers) in 1917. The 83rd Infantry Division's badge bears the four letters of the State of Ohio (the home state of most of its soldiers) embroidered one on top of the other on a black triangle.

A RED DIAMOND ON BOTH SIDES

The 5th US Division chose a red diamond as their emblem. This symbol was also chosen by the German 711th Infantry Division, which was stationed in Normandy between the Vallée de la Dives and the Seine estuary and defended the entire eastern sector of the Landing beaches.

HEER INFANTRYMAN/ MEDIC ASSISTANT

This soldier was an ordinary infantryman responsible for carrying wounded soldiers from his unit on stretchers. His white armband, which bears the words "Hilfs Krankenträger" meaning stretcher-bearer, instantly identifies him. As he was not an actual medic looking after the wounded, his helmet does not bear a red cross. He is wearing a regulation Heer rucksack which has been adapted to carry first aid material and bandages. He still has his basic military equipment but is also wearing two additional large capacity flasks with their specific straps. He is wearing a strong canvas strap around his neck that would have been used to help bear the weight of the stretcher.

THOUSANDS OF WOUNDED SOLDIERS

The Germans' individual bandages were generally wrapped in small packages, tied with a piece of string.

This German oxygen device transport box contained a bottle of oxygen, various flexible connectors and pipes, masks and connecting accessories.

Each medic carried a special case containing everything needed to treat minor wounds or bandage those who were more seriously injured while waiting to transfer them to a field hospital. The medic wore a white helmet and an armband bearing the Red Cross. A large flag, packed inside the case, was also used to try to protect the wounded and medics from harm.

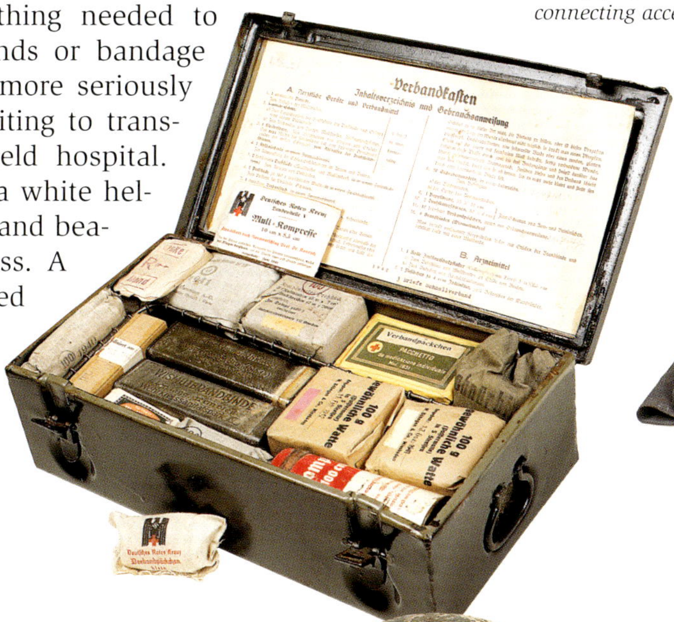

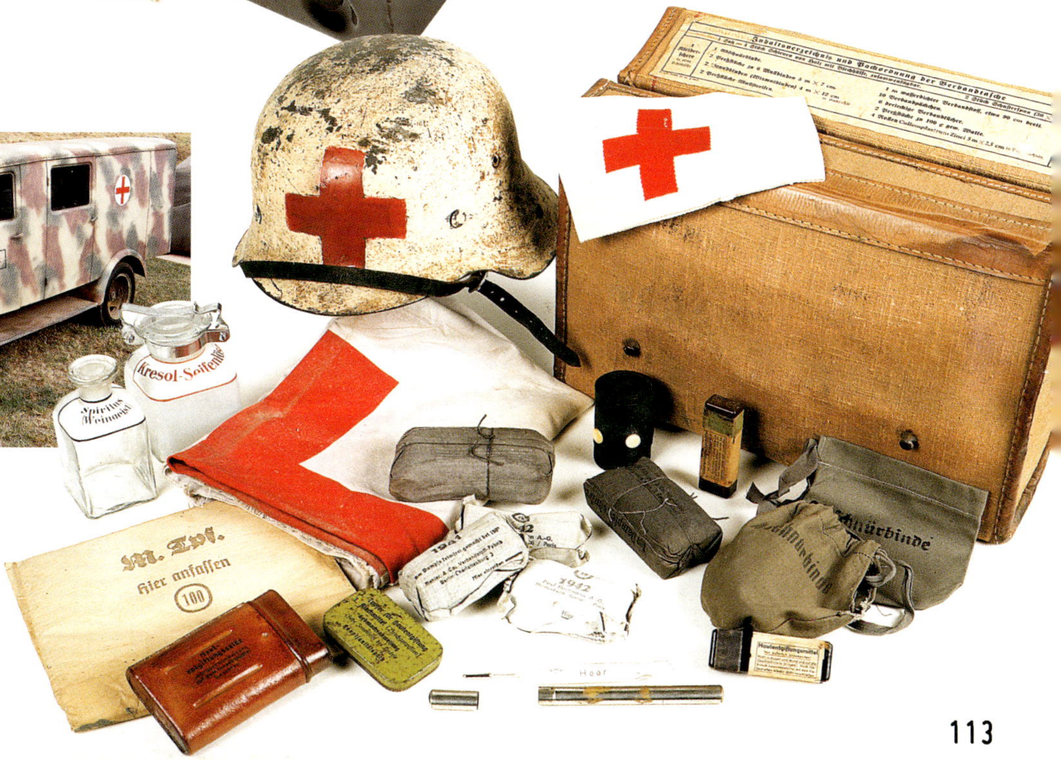

A MILITARY POLICE OFFICER FROM THE CANADIAN 1ST ARMY

The Allies set up a large security service to manage the increasing traffic coming from the beaches and Mulberry harbour, Arromanches-les-Bains. These military police officers, whether American, British or Canadian, like this one here, were given authority over all staff, from ordinary soldiers to four-star generals. This police corporal from the Canadian Provost Corps of the Canadian 1st Army is wearing a BD jacket with a "Provost" armband and a white Provost belt and shoulder strap. He is wearing a special Despatch Rider motorbike helmet and is carrying his rubber raincoat in his hand. He has slipped a signalling batton (a German model recovered from the field) and gauntlets inside his belt. The Canadian Provosts rode Harley Davidson or Norton motorbikes.

A FULLY MOTORISED ARMADA

The US Army was the first military organisation in the world to be fully motorised while, at the time, European armies still relied heavily on horse-drawn traction. Any army formed in America – the birthplace of the modern day automotive industry – had to move on wheels.
Motorisation also developed on the British side, albeit somewhat tardily. At the start of the war, the British automotive fleet included approx. 85,000 vehicles. Five years later, a spectacular 1,125,000 vehicles transported His Majesty's Army to the Berlin gates. This development can be explained by the fact that at first, the USA supplied the English with vehicles that had been ordered by the French before the war. It was not until later on that the British began producing their own vehicles with backing from Canada which had the advantage of manufacturing "very British" vehicles. Canada had an advantage over the USA – which also helped to equip the British troops – as Canadian vehicles fully complied with the specificities of British vehicles.

WILLYS OVERLAND JEEP

Length: 11ft. / Width: 5ft.
Height: 6ft. / Weight 1.1 tons
Maximum speed: 65mph
Cruising range: 236 miles
Armour: none
Engine: Willys Overland
Model: 4-cylinder MB
Displacement: 2,200cc
Horsepower: 60hp at 3,800rpm
Fuel consumption: 21mpg
Number of models manufactured:
Willys: 360,000
Ford: 260,000

DODGE WC 62

Length: 18ft
Width: 6ft
Height: 7ft
Weight: 3.2 tons
Maximum speed: 50mph
Range: 211 miles
Armour: none
Engine: Dodge
Model: 6-cylinder T 223
Displacement: 3,800cc
Horsepower: 92hp at 3,200rpm
Fuel consumption: 10mpg
Number of models manufactured: 43,278

THE STRENGTH OF THE ALLIES: TENS OF THOUSANDS OF VEHICLES AND THOUSANDS OF GALONS OF FUEL

The "Red Ball Convoy" for supplies...

The advancing Allied troops required thousands of tons of supplies each day. Once these supplies had been unloaded onto the beaches they needed to be transported as close as possible to the fighting. The Allies developed the "Red Ball Convoy", a simple yet effective system. This road, which had one northbound lane and one southbound lane, was reserved exclusively for HGVs which drove along it day and night at set speed limits. The HGVs were not allowed to stop or hinder the convoy and any vehicle which broke down was mercilessly pushed aside. The inexorable strength of the Allies stemmed from the fact that they had tens of thousands of vehicles, kept available for use, repaired and upgraded if necessary, and also from the fact that they had a virtually endless supply of fuel.

GMC DUKW 353

Length: 31ft. / Width: 8ft.
Height: 9ft. / Weight: 6.5 tons
Max. speed: 50mph
Cruising range: 239 miles
Armour: none
Engine: G.M.C.
Model: 6-cylinder 270
Displacement: 4,400cc
Horsepower: 104hp at 2,750rpm
Fuel consumption: 7mpg
Number of models manufactured: 21,147

...and "Pluto" for fuel

To transport the thousands of gallons of petrol required for their vehicles, the Allies called to "Pluto" for help. This Pluto had nothing to do with Mickey Mouse's yellow dog with large, floppy ears, but was instead an underwater pipeline running from the Isle of Wight to Arromanches-les-Bains harbour. From the first day of the Landings, huge floating reels were towed by tugboats, unrolling giant cables which sank to the bottom of the seabed before thousands of gallons of petrol were pumped through them. "Pluto" in fact stands for "Pipe-Line Under The Ocean". Engineers set up a huge network of pipes from the Arromanches-les-Bains harbour, which followed the Allied troops as they advanced and brought fuel as close as possible to the troops fighting at the front, right as far as Holland.

HALF-TRACK M3 A1

Length: 20ft. / Width: 7ft.
Height: 8ft. / Weight: 6.9 tons
Max. speed: 45mph
Cruising range: 199 miles
Armour: 0.3 to 0.5 inches
Engine: White
Type: 6-cylinder 160 AX
Displacement: 6,300cc
Horsepower: 147hp at 3,000rpm
Fuel consumption: 4mpg
Number of models manufactured: 41,170

G.M.C. CCKW-353

Length: 21ft. / Width: 7ft.
Height: 9ft. / Weight: 4.5 tons
Max. speed: 47mph
Cruising range: 240 miles
Armour: none
Engine: GMC / Model: 6-cylinder 270
Displacement: 4,400cc / Horsepower: 105hp at 2,750rpm
Fuel consumption: 7.5mpg
Number of models manufactured: 562,750

THOUSANDS OF SOLDIERS TRIED TO FLEE...

This "Heer Panzer Grenadier" is wearing a camouflaged smock over his woollen cloth uniform. His tired face shows his fear at the thought of being caught in an impossible situation. He was one of an army of 20,000 men – at least what was left of it – which, along with its weapons and equipment, had been completely surrounded by the Allies who were gradually and relentlessly closing in. The collar patches, which can be seen beneath his camouflaged smock, identify him as a Heer "Panzer Grenadier".

AN ENTIRE ARMY SURROUNDED

The German Seventh Army and the 5th Panzer Division tried to escape from the surrounding Allied armies made up of Americans in the south, British in the west, Canadians and Polish in the north and French soldiers from General Leclerc's 2nd Armoured Division. The French, who had landed at the start of August, rushed to close in on the area to which 150,000 men were fleeing with thousands of vehicles. On 21 August 1944, the Allied army closed in around the triangular area formed by the villages of Trun, Chambois and Saint Lambert-sur-Dive. 50,000 soldiers from all units of the Wehrmacht and Waffen-SS, 400 tanks, 2,000 vehicles and over 1,000 guns were completely surrounded. Due to a lack of organisation on the part of the Allies stemming from the rapidity of the operation, their ambush collapsed and over 100,000 Germans managed to escape from the enclosed area between 12 and 20 August. These soldiers were gradually discovered as they made their way to Berlin. The event which ought to have instantly brought an end to the War had failed. 240,000 men and over 30,000 vehicles managed to cross the Seine around Rouen a few days later in an attempt to regroup in Germany. The only consolation for the Allies, who helplessly watched the enemy escape, was that the Germans only managed to save 150 tanks.

The annihilation of the German troops caught in the "Corridor of Death" was so extreme that the remains of the battle could be found in the surrounding fields, woods and roads for several decades after the event. The carcasses of tanks and all sorts of vehicles, piles of equipment, hulls and oddly shaped pieces of metal bear witness to the severity of the event which brought an end to the Battle of Normandy in one fell swoop and more or less sealed the fate of the Third Reich Army.

THE TURNING POINT OF THE WAR...

The Battle of Normandy ended on 20 August 1944 on D+75, 15 days earlier than expected by the Allied High Command. During the period from D-Day to the closing of the Falaise Gap, the Germans lost 450,000 men, of which 200,000 were killed. 55 divisions were reduced to nothing. 1,500 tanks, 2,000 guns and 20,000 vehicles of all kinds were put out of action. Officers also suffered heavily and 23 unit commanders were killed, wounded (including Field Marshal Rommel himself) or taken prisoner.
75 days of uninterrupted fighting took the Allied troops from the Landing beaches to the banks of the River Seine.

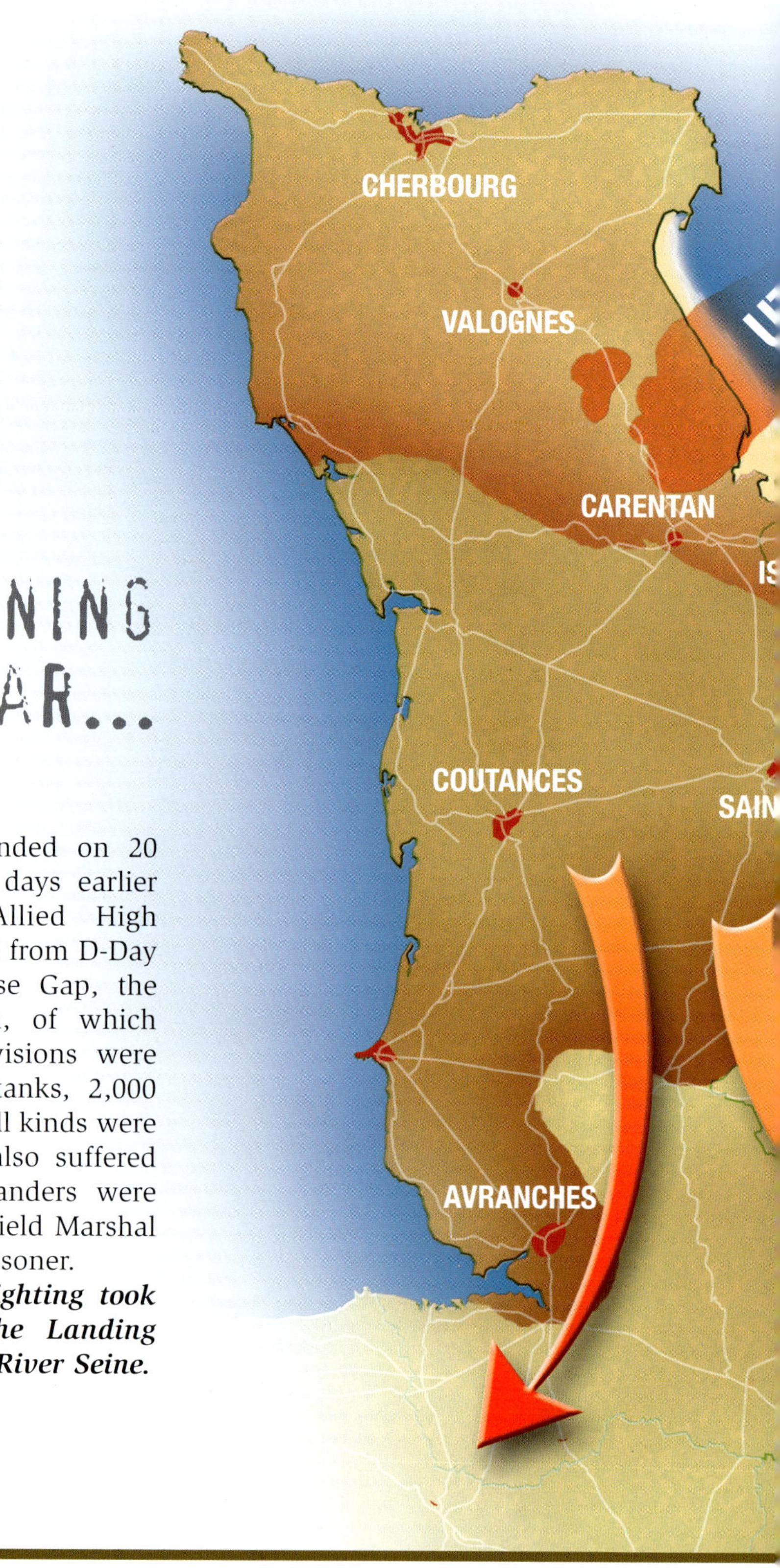

OMAHA
GOLD
JUNO
SWORD
LE HAVRE
TROUVILLE-SUR-MER
R-MER
BAYEUX
OUISTREHAM
CABOURG
CAEN
LISIEUX
FALAISE
CHAMBOIS
ARGENTAN

... AND TENS OF THOUSANDS OF DEATHS

FAMOUS OR ANONYMOUS...

Tens of thousands of soldiers are buried in Normandy soil in the anonymous rows of graves marked with white crosses, stone slabs or terracotta blocks. The British often buried their dead on the spot in 16 cemeteries scattered throughout the Normandy bocage. 40 graves can be found in Chouain-Jerusalem, the smallest British cemetery. Canadian soldiers are buried in two cemeteries, one in Bény-Réviers and one in Bretteville-sur-Laize, and 650 Polish soldiers are buried in Grainville-Langannerie. The Americans buried those soldiers whose families wished their bodies to remain in France in two cemeteries (Saint-James and Colleville-Saint-Laurent). German soldiers killed in the Normandy battles are buried in 6 cemeteries, the largest of which is La Cambe with 21,200 graves. This cemetery is located between Bayeux and Isigny, and bodies recovered from the Normandy countryside sixty years later are still buried here today.

UNITED FOR ETERNITY

They were always buried in fives. Whether British, Polish, German or American, they fought the war inside steel monsters. When death struck, they were often united for eternity. Tank crews were therefore buried in communal graves, mounted with a slab bearing their five names, just as in the days when tank commander, gun-layer, gunner, artillery-man and driver worked together as one.

Among all the anonymous crews, one grave is more colourful and famous than the others. It is that of the crew of Tiger # 007 under Hauptman Michaël Wittmann.

They were brothers. Together they donned a soldier's uniform to help put an end to that dirty war which was raging through old Europe and beginning to engulf the rest of the world. In a tragic blow of fate they were killed and laid to rest in peace, side by side. Read on to discover the terrible yet incredible story of eight brothers who all died at war.

"BROTHERS IN ARMS"

Killed the same day, in the same unit...

The Hoback brothers from the State of Virginia chose to sign up together to the 116th Infantry Regiment which was part of the "Blue and Grey" 29th Infantry Division. This unit's objective was to get a foothold on the beach codenamed "Omaha Beach". What they did not yet know was that their division and, in particular, their regiment was to come under a hail of enemy fire and suffer heavy losses. PVT Bedford T. Hoback and Staff Sergeant Raymond S. Hoback were mowed down in the attack. T. Hoback's body is buried in grave G 10 28 in the American cemetery in Colleville-sur-Mer. The body of his brother Raymond was never recovered, but his name is engraved on the cemetery's "Wall of the Missing".

Killed the same day, by the same shell...

The Moreland brothers came from the small village of Bushong near Lyon in the State of Kansas. They signed up to the same unit, the 149th Engineer Combat Battalion, where Jay B. was Sergeant and his brother, William W. had the slightly higher rank of Staff Sergeant. On the morning of 6 June 1944, the brothers were on board LCI 92, an infantry landing craft heading for Omaha Beach. The engineer battalion was due to land with the second wave of attack and had the task of demolishing obstacles and clearing them out of the way. The ship, which was making its way through the various obstacles and debris which had begun to accumulate in the water in front of the beach, hit a mine which exploded underneath the hull, bringing the ship to a standstill. The ship was then hit full blast by a shell, which instantly killed dozens of soldiers who were waiting to land. Both brothers were killed in one of the ship's compartments. Their bodies were in such a bad state that the American authorities took several years to identify them. By consecutive crosschecking, the authorities were able to establish that grave X 53 which, up to that point had contained the body of an unknown soldier, could possibly be that of Sergeant Jay B. Moreland. The name of "Staff Sergeant" William W. Moreland can still be seen on the "Wall of the Missing".

Killed the same day, on two different beaches...

The brothers Joseph and Manuel Arruda from Massachusetts were both first class soldiers assigned to two different units. The elder brother, Joseph, signed up to the 8th Infantry Regiment which was part of the "Ivy" 4th Division. His brother Manuel, on the other hand, fought with the famous 1st Division or the "Big Red One" as part of the 1st Engineer Combat Battalion. On 6 June 1944, PFC Joseph F. Arruda landed on Utah Beach. Nineteen miles further east, his brother Manuel landed on Omaha beach. As part of the engineering unit, his task was to demolish any obstacles that defended the beach preventing the next wave of attack from landing. However, as irony had it, the soldiers landing on Utah beach met with little resistance whereas Omaha beach became known as "Bloody Omaha". Two beaches with two different destinies and yet the two brothers met the same fate. On the evening of 6 June, their names were added to the long list of victims of the first day of the invasion. They are both buried in the American cemetery in Colleville-sur-Mer, and lie side by side in graves G 5 25 and G 5 26.

The real "Private Ryan"

Preston and Robert Niland came from the State of New York and it was their story that was to inspire Steven Spielberg's film, "Saving Private Ryan". Robert J. Niland was a Sergeant in the 82nd Airborne Division, which, along with the 101st Airborne Division, was one of the USA's most famous parachute units. Robert was therefore one of the first soldiers to land on Normandy soil together with his comrades from the 505th Parachute Infantry Regiment. He was also one of the first victims. His brother Preston T. was 2nd Lieutenant in the 22nd Infantry Regiment which formed part of the 4th Division. This division landed on Utah Beach a few miles away from the area where the 82nd Airborne paratroopers had landed. The Lieutenant must certainly have been unaware of his brother's fate when he too was killed the next day. The brothers are buried in the American cemetery of Colleville-sur-Mer. They are buried side by side in graves F 15 11 and F 15 12.

TABLE OF CONTENTS

ACKNOWLEDGEMENTS

My thanks go out to everyone who so warmly and kindly lent their support during the creation of this book.

I am particularly grateful to Tanguy Le Sant and François Lepetit for having made contacts, and building relationships with the museums and private collectors over the months.

Without their help and collections this project would never have made it to the printing press.

I would also like to thank all those who so warmly welcomed, supported and encouraged me during my work:

the Museums and their curators,

Daniel Trefeu from the Omaha museum in Saint-Laurent-sur-Mer,

Pierre-Louis Gosselin from the Big Red One Assault Museum,

Auguste Foché and President Jean d'Aigneaux from Musée Airborne in Sainte-Mère-Eglise,

Michel Brissard from Musée D.Day Omaha at Vierville-sur-Mer and his Mulberry reconstruction project,

Eric Pasturel from Musée Remember in Dinan, for his kindness and commitment,

M. Tisserand, caretaker of the German military cemetery of La Cambe,

Marie-France and Ronald Hirlé from Editions Hirlé in Strasbourg, for their help and for giving me access to their archives,

François Cibulski, Charles-Hubert, Philippe and Romuald for their passion for history,

and last but not least, two enthusiastic collectors who so patiently and kindly shared their collections with me but who prefer to remain anonymous. They'll know who I mean.

The scale models of tanks, vehicles and aircraft were provided by true craftsmen who so kindly lent their support to the illustration of this book and I would particularly like to thank:

François Lepetit for the Centaur IV and Cromwell IV on page 59, the Churchill Crocodile on page 60, the group of Shermans and the Pacific with its tank trailer on page 61, the Sherman "Hedge Cutter" on page 96, the Tiger on page 97, the Panther on page 99 and the German vehicles on page 101.

Pascal Lejouis for the models and Frédéric Mouchel for the dioramas of the LCM on page 39, the Sherman tank on page 59, the Sherman Duplex Drive and Flail on page 60, the Destroyer M10 on page 61 and the Panther G on page 100.

Michel Tonnevy for the Spitfire on page 67.

I am extremely grateful to AMAC 35, the model makers club in Cesson-Sévigné, France, who helped me enormously with this project and helped me contact the model makers.

Franck Bazin, President of AMAC 35, for the Panzer IV on page 101.

Jean-Christophe Josse for the Typhoon on page 67.

All the badges shown belong to the Editions Hirlé collection.

PARTICIPATING MUSEUMS

The items used to illustrate this book belong to private collectors and museums which willingly took part in this project. Bearing witness to our history, these objects deserve to be 'seen for real', as photographs can only partly capture some of the emotion surrounding them. The museums that they belong to successfully display these objects, along with many others, within the framework of their historical setting, and you will be moved as you discover their story.

MUSEE OMAHA

Musée mémorial d'Omaha Beach
Les Moulins, avenue de la Libération,
14710 Saint-Laurent-sur-Mer
France

Tel. +33 (0)2 31 21 97 44
Fax: +33 (0)2 31 92 72 80

Email: musee-memorial-omaha@wanadoo.fr
Website: www.musee-memorial-omaha.com

Opening times:
15/02 - 15/03: 10-12.30am and 2.30-6pm
16/03 - 15/05: 9.30am - 6.30pm
16/05 - 15/09: 9.30am - 7pm
except for July - August: 9.30am - 7.30pm
16/09 - 15/11: 9.30am - 6.30pm.

The museum displays a superb collection of military vehicles, weapons, uniforms and badges worn by American and German soldiers during the Second World War and portrays events and life under German occupation. Documents about the Resistance and deportation are exhibited and translated into English. There is also a life-size panorama with models of troops in combat, depicting the fighting on Omaha beach during the landings.

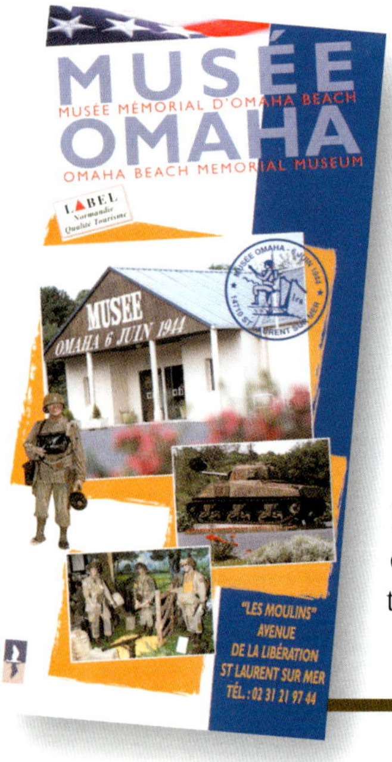

MUSEE REMEMBER 1939 - 1945

Le Pont de la Haye
Léhon - 22100 Dinan
France

Tel. +33 (0)2 96 39 65 89

Opening times:
Everyday during school holidays
and bank holidays:
10-12am and 1.30-6.30pm
Off-season: by appointment

A display of over 2,000 war items, from cigarette packets to aircraft engines, with over 20 dummies dressed in original clothing, guns and war vehicles. Exhibition dedicated to the Resistance movement fighters with tracts, parachute containers and S.A.S. objects. Reconstruction of a German bunker complete with barrack-room, regulation equipment, radio room and armoury. The gunroom armed with a 47mm Skoda gun is the only one of its kind in Europe.

BIG RED ONE ASSAULT MUSEUM

Mr Pierre-Louis Gosselin.
Hameau Le Bray - D514
14710 Colleville-sur-Mer - Omaha Beach
France

Tel. +33 (0) 2 31 21 53 81 / +33 (0)6 72 89 36 18

Opening times:
01/03 – 31/05: 10am - 6pm
01/06 – 31/08: 9am - 7pm
01/09 – 30/11: 10am - 6pm
Closed in December, January and February.

This museum focuses in particular on the first waves of attack of the American Infantry on Omaha Beach on 6 June 1944. It covers aspects of their training, boarding the landing craft in Great Britain and the participation of the 1st and 29th US divisions in the Liberation of Normandy. There is an exhibition of equipment, weapons, dummies and rare war items and the museum also boasts archives of photographs and letters. Disabled access. Private car park for coaches and cars.

MUSEE AIRBONE

Musée des troupes aéroportées
et du Doublas C-47
(Airborne troops and Douglas C-47 museum)
50480 Sainte-Mère-Eglise, France

Tel. +33 (0)2 33 41 41 35
Fax: +33 (0)2 33 44 78 87

Email: musee.airborne@wanadoo.fr
Website: www. Airborne-museum.org

Opening times:
01/02 - 30/11: every day

The first museum building is set in the middle of a large park and is designed in the shape of a parachute. It houses an authentic Waco glider and various displays of documents and objects from the period including weapons, ammunition, equipment and uniforms. The second building displays a Douglas C-47 which dropped paratroopers and towed gliders during the Overlord operation. Various dummies in period uniforms are displayed as well as personal memorabilia donated by American veterans. Interactive terminals throughout the rooms help visitors to discover more about the Liberation of Sainte-Mère-Eglise and the Battle of Normandy.

MUSEE D.DAY OMAHA

Route de Grandcamp
14710 Vierville-sur-Mer - France

Tel. and Fax: +33 (0)2 31 21 71 80

Opening times:
01/04 - 31/05: 10am - 12.30pm and 2pm - 6pm
01/06 - 30/09: 9.30am - 7.30pm
01/10 - 11/11: 10am - 12.30pm and 2pm - 6pm

An outstanding collection of vehicles, weapons, uniforms and equipment tells the story of four years of German Occupation and the Landings as experienced by the 1st American Infantry Division on Omaha beach.

Editor: Servane Biguais
Design and layout: Ad Lib, Rennes, France
Photoengraving: Micro Lynx, France
Printing: Gibert Clarey Imprimeurs, Chambray-lès-Tours (37)

I.S.B.N.: 978-2-7373-3404-7 - Publisher no.: 4650.08.01.03.14
Legal deposit: April 2004. Printed in France.
www.editionsouestfrance.fr